THE GUIDE TO LAUGHING®
at
FAMILY

GTL Institute Member Handbook

1st Edition

THE GUIDE TO LAUGHING AT FAMILY
GTL INSTITUTE MEMBER HANDBOOK
1ST EDITION

Executive Editor ·· Shawn Gold
Copy Editor ··· Joe Marich
Assistant Editor ··································· Caroline Applegate
Assistant Editor ···································· Christina Carrillo
Assistant Editor ·· Ryan Joe

Book Design ··· Digital Soup
Illustration ··· Don Anderson
Conceptual Design ····································· Randy Horton
Producer ··· Margie Gilmore
Spaghetti Wall ······················· Marc Shaiman & Scott Wittman

Library of Congress Control Number: 2004102265
ISBN 0-9729636-2-6
Typeset in House Industries Chalet™ and Sign Painter™ Families
Printed in Canada

Distributed in North America by CDS Books
425 Madison Avenue
New York, 10017

Published by Handy Logic Press
8033 Sunset Blvd, #490
Los Angeles, CA 90046

10 9 8 7 6 5 4 3 2 1

The "insightful observations" in this book were gathered enthusiastically but
unscientifically over many years and contributed by hundreds of friends and
acquaintances. Some arrived on cocktail napkins, phone answering machines,
emails and through conversations. Every effort was made to be exact in re-
telling the observations contained herein, but inevitably mistakes were made.
To the original sources and contributors, our sincere gratitude, and where
appropriate, our sincere apologies. Please contact us at Handy Logic Press with
any corrections and we will do our best to make those changes in subsequent
editions.

Table of Contents

CHILDHOOD, cont.

The Power of Laughter

Laughter is an innate reaction we have as humans and its potency with regard to our well-being is undeniable. Dating as far back as ancient Greece, hospitals were built next to amphitheatres because the "mirth" of the audience was thought to heal patients. Even the Book of Proverbs in the Old Testament contains verses like "A cheerful heart is as good as medicine, but a downcast spirit dries up the bones."

Laughter is irrefutably contagious and many times more powerful when shared. A funny situation shared among friends is immensely more enjoyable than when experienced alone. The power of laughter's contagion is illustrated everywhere from the collective snickers of children in a classroom to the use of television laugh tracks to elicit laughter from the viewing audience.

In his 1979 autobiography, *Anatomy of an Illness*, Norman Cousins brought the issue of humor therapy to the attention of the medical community. Cases like his, in which laughter therapy brought terminally ill patients to good health, helped popularize the subject. But it wasn't until 1989—when the *Journal of the American Medical Association (JAMA)* acknowledged that laughter helps improve the quality of life for patients with chronic illnesses—that laughter therapy was recognized as a legitimate form of treatment, which brings immediate, symptom-relieving effects. This initiated studies around the world, essentially proving that mirth strengthens, and negative emotions like depression and anger weaken the immune system. Today, the effects of laughter are considered a powerful weapon in the fight against AIDS, cancer, and other diseases.

For even the healthiest people, laughter is needed to maintain wellness both mentally and physically. The stress and strain of conflicts and tension around us can compound our everyday concerns, contributing to a rise in anxiety and depression. For overall wellness, laughter therapy takes on its biggest responsibility: preventing illness by providing a daily release for the body's negative energies and allowing us to focus on the positive.

6

The Mission

"WELLNESS THROUGH LAUGHTER"

The *Guide to Laughing Institute* recognizes the power of laughter and is doing its part to create a sense of wellness and perspective in the world. Our intention is to help people laugh and learn about life and to connect with each other through shared laughter.

To this end, we continue to collect humorous and "insightful observations" about life from around the world and present them in a fun, concise and sharable format. The *GTL Institute* member handbooks serve as a no-nonsense guide to laughing at life and putting problems in perspective. They are designed as an aid to help people discover the lighter side of life's issues, communicate those findings, and connect with others—and to laugh, snicker, giggle, chuckle, cackle, snort, hoot and guffaw.

Let us be grateful to people who make us happy: they are the charming gardeners who make our souls BLOSSOM.

MARCEL PROUST (1871–1922)
FRENCH NOVELIST

Insightful Observations

The Guide to Laughing Institute honors those selected to be in this book for their wit and wisdom, for helping others laugh and learn about FAMILY, and for the impact they have had on our culture.

Their insightful observations have been selected based on the unique perspective they offer, for how concisely they convey wit and wisdom on a given subject, and for their balance of humor, irony, and the unvarnished truth.

Because insightful humor comes in many forms, the observations contained herein are broken out into three primary viewpoints: the **IDEALIST**, the **REALIST**, and the **CYNIC**. Next to each observation, you will see an icon or emoticon that denotes the attitude and perspective of the expert, as it relates to the topic:

 The Idealist: An optimist, one who is predisposed to a positive outcome; the Idealist finds humor in picturesque fantasies and delights in romantic expectations.

 The Realist: One who is inclined to finding a literal truth. They enjoy humor that sheds light on a practical way of approaching or assessing a situation or of solving a problem.

 The Cynic: One who instinctively questions or disagrees with assertions or generally accepted conclusions. A person of wit, who negatively focuses on the incongruities of life and seems to enjoy it.

Humor is just another defense against the Universe.

MEL BROOKS (1926–) WRITER, PRODUCER, DIRECTOR

Member Obligations

ENJOY LIFE

It is more important to have fun than to be funny. Laughter is not so much about jokes as it is about being playful and finding the humor in everyday life. As we mature, life's issues can overwhelm us, causing us to enjoy less and stress more. It is commonly recognized that adults laugh around fifteen times a day, while children laugh *several hundred* times a day. Because laughter in children is so closely associated with play, it is thought that adults laugh less than children simply because they play less. As a *GTL Institute* member, you are charged with opening up to the humor in everyday experiences, recapturing the spirit of play, and celebrating life. By enjoying life, you will become contagious and will have a significant impact on the well-being of those around you.

SHARE LAUGHTER

The *GTL Institute* believes that the essence of life is to connect with people and that the key to connection is laughter. Making a *laughter connection* is one of the best ways to firm-up an old friendship or recognize a new one. It is a form of positive social interaction for every culture because it unites people based on the things they enjoy and the way they see life. Anyone can learn to share laughter and help others laugh. It does not mean telling jokes (unless this is one of your talents); it means sharing your humorous perspective and giving others permission to do the same. As you continue to laugh and learn about life, we hope you spread your newfound knowledge to others and join the *GTL Institute* in creating a circle of laughter and mirth.

I Agree _____
(member initials)

Laughter is the shortest distance between two people.

VICTOR BORGE (1909–2000) CLOWN PRINCE OF DENMARK

Step One:

HAV

BA

ING
BIES

Planning a Family

Pregnancy

Babies

HAVING BABIES

CHILDHOOD

TEENAGERS

PARENTING

HOME LIFE

RELATIVES

PLANNING A FAMILY

Insightful Observations on
REASONS TO HAVE A BABY

Babies are such a nice way to start people.

 Don Herrold
(1899-1966) Cartoonist, Humorist

The great gift of family life is to be intimately acquainted with people you might never even introduce yourself to, had life not done it for you.

Dave Barry
(1947-) Author, Humorist

Call it a clan, call it a network, call it a tribe, call it a family. Whatever you call it, whoever you are, you need one.

 Jane Howard
(1935-1996) Journalist, Writer

The reason most people have kids is because they get pregnant.

Barbara Kingsolver
(1955-) Writer

I get those maternal feelings, like when I'm lying on the couch and can't reach the remote. "Boy, a kid would be nice right now."

Kathleen Madigan
Present Day Comedian, Actor

My biological clock is ticking so loudly I'm nearly deafened by it. They search me going into planes.

Marian Keyes
(1963-) Irish Novelist

I'd like to have kids one day, though. I want to be called Mommy by someone other than guys in the street.

 Carol Leifer
(1956-) Comedian, Writer, Actress, Producer,

THE GUIDE TO LAUGHING AT FAMILY

PLANNING A FAMILY

Insightful Observations on
DECIDING TO HAVE ONE

HAVING BABIES

CHILDHOOD

TEENAGERS

PARENTING

HOME LIFE

RELATIVES

Having a child is surely the most beautifully irrational act that two people in love can commit.

 Bill Cosby
(1937-) Comedian, Actor

I'd get pregnant if I could be assured I'd have puppies.

 Cynthia Nelms
Author, Humorist

It was the tiniest thing I ever decided to put my whole life into.

 Author Unknown

Making the decision to have a child is momentous. It is to decide forever to have your heart go walking around outside your body.

 Elizabeth Stone
Present Day Author

Family is a mixed blessing. You're glad to have one, but it's also like receiving a sentence for a crime you didn't commit.

 Rita Rudner
(1956-) Comedian

Everyone should have kids. They are the greatest joy in the world. But they are also terrorists. You'll realize this as soon as they are born, and they start using sleep deprivation to break you.

 Ray Romano
(1957-) Actor, Comedian

 = IDEALIST = REALIST  = CYNIC

13

PLANNING A FAMILY

Insightful Observations on FAMILY PLANNING

Never have children, only grandchildren.

Gore Vidal
(1925-) Novelist, Playwright, Essayist

CHARLOTTE: I promise I won't become one of those mothers who can only talk about diaper genies.
CARRIE: Good.
SAMANTHA: What the hell is a diaper genie?
CARRIE: I don't know...someone you hire to change a kid's diaper?

Kristin Davis, Sarah Jessica Parker, and Kim Cattrall
in HBO's *Sex and the City*

Have children while your parents are still young enough to take care of them.

Rita Rudner
(1956-) Comedian

Parenthood is a lot easier to get into than get out of.

Bruce Lansky
Present Day Poet, Writer

The time not to become a father is eighteen years before a war.

E.B. White
(1899-1985) American Author, Humorist

My husband and I are either going to buy a dog or have a child. We can't decide whether to ruin our carpet or ruin our lives.

Rita Rudner
(1956-)Comedian

I can't believe I forgot to have children!

Roy Lichtenstein
(1923-1997) Painter; **caption from painting**

14

PLANNING A FAMILY

Insightful Observations on
PREPARING YOURSELF

I think of birth as a search for a larger apartment.

Rita Mae Brown
(1944-) Writer

It sometimes happens, even in the best of families, that a baby is born. This is not necessarily cause for alarm. The important thing is to keep your wits about you and borrow some money.

Elinor Goulding Smith
(1917-1978) Author, Humorist

Ideally they should give you a couple of "practice kids" before you have any for real. Sort of like bowling a few frames for free before you start keeping score. Let you warm up.

Paul Reiser
(1957-) Actor, Writer, Comedian

Though motherhood is the most important of all the professions—requiring more knowledge than any other department in human affairs—there was no attention given to preparation for this office.

Elizabeth Cady Stanton
(1815-1902) Suffragette, Abolitionist

For fathers-to-be, pregnancy serves as a time of profound transition: nine months of mental, emotional, material, perhaps physical, and almost certainly financial preparation to become a father.

Kevin Osborn
Present Day Author; *The Complete Idiot's Guide to Fatherhood*

Literature is mostly about having sex and not much about having children; life is the other way around.

David Lodge
(1935-) Novelist, Critic

PLANNING A FAMILY

Insightful Observations on
FEELING UNPREPARED

Parenthood remains the greatest single preserve of the amateur.

 Alvin Toffler
(1928-) American Futurist, Author

Babies are always more trouble than you thought—and more wonderful.

 Charles Osgood
(1933-) Broadcast Journalist

Most of us become parents long before we have stopped being children.

 Mignon McLaughlin
(1915-) Author, Journalist

Who of us is mature enough for offspring before the offspring themselves arrive? The value of marriage is not that adults produce children but that children produce adults.

 Peter DeVries
(1910-1993) Editor, Writer

There are two things in life for which we are never fully prepared. Twins.

 Josh Billings
(1818-1885) Humorist

The moment a child is born, the mother is also born. She never existed before. The woman existed, but the mother, never. A mother is something absolutely new.

 Rajneesh
20th Century Spiritual Writer

16

HAVING BABIES

CHILDHOOD

TEENAGERS

PARENTING

HOME LIFE

RELATIVES

PLANNING A FAMILY

Insightful Observations on AVOIDING CHILDREN

HAVING BABIES

CHILDHOOD

TEENAGERS

PARENTING

HOME LIFE

RELATIVES

I've always, always wanted to give birth. To kittens. I figure it would hurt less, and when you're done, you'd have kittens!

Betsy Salkind
Present Day Actress, Comedian, Writer

It's tough, if you just want a little creature you can love, you can get a puppy.

Barbara Walters
(1931-) News Correspondent, Actress, Producer

When asked why he did not become a father, Thales answered, "Because I am fond of children."

Diogenes Laertius
(c. 150 B.C.) Biographer of Ancient Greek Philosophers

Families with babies and families without babies feel sorry for each other.

Ed Howe
(1853-1937) Editor, Novelist, Essayist

I'll never have a baby because I'm afraid I'll leave it on top of my car.

Lizz Winstead
(1961-) Political Comic, Writer

SAMANTHA: Frankly, I think it's sad, the way she's using a child to validate her existence. CARRIE: Exactly. Why can't she just use sex and a nice cocktail like the rest of us.

Kim Catrell and Sarah Jessica Parker
in HBO's *Sex and the City*

Learning to dislike children at an early age saves a lot of expense and aggravation later in life.

Robert Byrne
(1930-) Author, Humorist

INSIGHTFUL OBSERVATIONS TO SHARE

17

PLANNING A FAMILY

Insightful Observations on OLDER MOTHERS

I'll try anything once.

Alice Roosevelt Longworth
(1884-1980) Author; **on giving birth at age 41**

According to author Sylvia Hewlitt, career women shouldn't wait to have a baby because our fertility takes a steep drop-off after age twenty-seven. Ladies, there's no reason to panic; either your cooter works or it doesn't. My mom had me when she was forty, and this was back in the '70s, when the only fertility aid was Harvey's Bristol Cream.

Tina Fey
(1970-) Comedian, Actress

I'm trying to understand this generation. They have adjusted the time table for childbearing so that menopause and teaching a sixteen-year-old how to drive will occur the same week.

Erma Bombeck
(1927-1996) Humorist, Author

All the other parents who have children my daughter's age are ten to twenty years younger than I am and are tattooed and pierced. When I meet them for a play date with our kids, I feel like I should be baby-sitting them too. "Where do you think you're going with hair that color, young man? That nipple ring is going to get infected."

Reno Goodale
Present Day Comedian

I read an article in a magazine: women 49 years old having their first child. Forty-nine! I couldn't think of a better way to spend my golden years. What's the advantage of having a kid at 49? So you can both be in diapers at the same time?

Sue Kolinsky
Modern Day Comedian

18

PLANNING A FAMILY

Insightful Observations on GETTING PREGNANT

HAVING BABIES

CHILDHOOD

TEENAGERS

PARENTING

HOME LIFE

RELATIVES

Pregnancy is amazing. To think that you can create a human being just with the things you have around the house.

 Shang
Present Day Comedian, Actor

I don't have any kids. Well, at least none that I know about.

 Carol Leifer
(1956-) Comedian, Writer, Actress, Producer,

When I was growing up, the fertility drug was alcohol.

 Kelly Monteith
(1942-) Actor, Writer, Comedian

My girlfriend Holly and I went to visit a friend who has two children. Afterward all Holly could talk about was how cute the kids were. That's pretty scary to a single guy. The only time scarier was when she was shaking the stick from the pregnancy kit, and I was yelling like I was at the roulette table in Vegas, "Come on blue! Come on blue!

 Joel Warshaw
Present Day Comedian

If it's so hard to get pregnant, how do you account for the number of crying children on planes?

 Kim Cattrall
in HBO's *Sex and the City*

 = IDEALIST   = REALIST   = CYNIC

HAVING BABIES

CHILDHOOD

TEENAGERS

PARENTING

HOME LIFE

RELATIVES

PREGNANCY

Insightful Observations on
BEING PREGNANT

If men had to have babies they would only ever have one each.

Diana, Princess of Wales
(1961-1998) Wife of Prince Charles

Q: The more pregnant I get, the more often strangers smile at me. Why?
A: 'Cause you're fatter than they are.

Author Unknown

I feel like a man building a boat in his basement which he may not be able to get out through the door. Trapped, frantic and trapped.

Abigail Lewis
Present Day Author

If pregnancy were a book they would cut the last two chapters.

Nora Ephron
(1941-) Writer, Director, Producer

When I had almost reached my term, I looked like a rat dragging a stolen egg.

Colette
(1873-1954) French Novelist

THE GUIDE TO LAUGHING AT FAMILY

PREGNANCY

Insightful Observations on
PREGNANCY WARNINGS

HAVING BABIES

CHILDHOOD

TEENAGERS

PARENTING

HOME LIFE

RELATIVES

None of the mothers of my generation quit smoking when they were pregnant. The philosophy then was "I'm smoking for two now.

Reno Goodale
Present Day Comedian

Now the thing about having a baby—and I can't be the first person to have noticed this—is that thereafter you have it.

Jean Kerr
(1922-2003) Writer,
Dramatist, Lyricist

They caution pregnant women not to drink alcohol. It may harm the baby. I think that's ironic. If it wasn't for alcohol most women wouldn't be that way.

Rita Rudner
(1956-) Comedian

My wife is petite, so for the first four months she wasn't showing. I thought she was faking it to get out of changing the cat litter. Because apparently that's a rule now; she showed me the book. "Look, Tom. It says that pregnant women shouldn't handle the cat litter for fear of toxoplasmosis!" "Wow, honey. Y'know what? I don't want toxoplasmosis either!" Women write those pregnancy books; they could put anything they want in there. "It says that pregnant women shouldn't...umm...wash dishes either. For fear of wrinkly-fingery-smosis.

Tom Pecora
Present Day Comedian

Do not name your child after a Scandinavian deity or any aspect of the weather.

Daniel Menaker
Present Day Author

PREGNANCY

Insightful Observations on WOMENS' BODIES

Think of stretch marks as pregnancy service stripes.

Joyce Armor
Present Day Writer

Ah, to be skinny herself! To sleep on her flat stomach, walk lightly again on the balls of her feet.

Doris Betts
(1932-) Author

The baby was a lovely little boy, but sad to say, he did not weigh sixty pounds. That is what I had gained and that was what I had to lose.

Barbara Bush
(1925-) Wife of 41st U.S. President George Bush Sr.

You must remember that when you are pregnant, you are eating for two. But you must also remember that the other one of you is the size of a golf ball, so let's not go overboard with it. I mean, a lot of pregnant women eat as though the other person they were eating for is Orson Welles.

Dave Barry
(1947-) Author Humorist; **referring to the extra large movie mogul**

By far the most common craving of pregnant women is not to be pregnant.

Phyllis Diller
(1917-) Comedian, Actress, Author

22

PREGNANCY

Insightful Observations on
DEALING WITH PREGNANT WOMEN

A pregnant woman wants toasted snow.

 Hebrew Proverb

You should never say anything to a woman that even remotely suggests that you think she's pregnant unless you can see an actual baby emerging from her at that moment.

 Dave Barry
(1947-) Author, Humorist

Q: My wife is five months pregnant and so moody that sometimes she's borderline irrational.
A: So what's your question?

 Internet Message Board For New Fathers

The biggest problem facing pregnant women is not nausea or fatigue or her wardrobe—it's free advice.

 Sophia Loren
(1934-) Actress, Sex Symbol

HAVING BABIES

CHILDHOOD

TEENAGERS

PARENTING

HOME LIFE

RELATIVES

PREGNANCY

Insightful Observations on THE UNBORN CHILD

Her child was like a load that held her down, and yet like a hand that pulled her to her feet.

 Edith Wharton
(1862-1937) Author, Poet

Little Fish, You kick and dart and glide Beneath my ribs, As if they were your private reef.

 Ethna McKiernan
20th Century Irish-American Poet

The sonogram. We had fun looking for early traces of family resemblance. "Gee, honey, it looks just like your mother, if she were bald, had no eyelids, and was floating in amniotic fluid." "Yeah, but from this side, it looks like your father. Presuming, of course, he was a Hawaiian prawn.

Paul Reiser
(1957-) Actor, Writer, Comedian

The baby bounced gently off the wall of her uterus. She opened her dressing gown and put her hands back on her belly. It moved again like a dolphin going through the water; that was the way she imagined it. "Are yeh normal?" she said.

 Roddy Doyle
(1958-) Irish Novelist, Playwright

The trouble with getting introspective when you're pregnant is that you never know who you might run into.

 Carrie Fisher
(1956-) Actress, Writer

Life is tough enough without having someone kick you from the inside.

Rita Rudner
(1956-) Comedian

24

PREGNANCY

Insightful Observations on
DELIVERY

HAVING BABIES

CHILDHOOD

TEENAGERS

PARENTING

HOME LIFE

RELATIVES

My mother groan'd, my father wept, Into the dangerous world I leapt.

William Blake
(1757-1827) British Poet

If God were a woman, She would have installed one of those turkey thermometers in our belly buttons. When we were done, the thermometer pops up, the doctor reaches for the zipper conveniently located beneath our bikini lines, and out comes a smiling, fully diapered baby.

Candice Bergen
(1946-) Actress

"Delivery" is the wrong word to describe the childbearing process. Deliver is: "Here's your pizza. Takes thirty minutes or less." "Exorcism," I think, is more apt: "Please! Get the hell out of my body!"

Jeff Stilson
(1959-) Comedian, Writer, Producer

Hard Labor: A redundancy, like "working mother."

Joyce Armor
Present Day Writer

These wretched babies don't come until they are ready.

Elizabeth II
(1926-) Queen of England

Having a baby is like taking your lower lip and forcing it over your head.

Carol Burnett
(1933-) Actress, Comedian, Singer, Director, Producer, Writer

My sister was in labor for thirty-six hours. Ow. She got wheeled out of delivery, looked at me, and said, "Adopt."

Caroline Rhea
(1964-) Actor, Writer, Comedian

 = IDEALIST  = REALIST   = CYNIC

25

HAVING BABIES

CHILDHOOD

TEENAGERS

PARENTING

HOME LIFE

RELATIVES

PREGNANCY

Insightful Observations on
PAIN RELIEF

It's all about having a GOOD TIME.

Dr. William Wright
20th Century Obstetrical
Anasthesiology Pioneer

I'm not interested in being Wonder Woman in the delivery room. Give me drugs.

Madonna
(1958-) Singer, SongWriter,
Children's Book Author

You take Lamaze classes. I went. It was a total waste of time. Ain't nobody going to breathe a baby out. There's going to be a fight.

Sinbad
(1956-) Comedian, Actor,
Writer

I want to have children, but my friends scare me. One of my friends told me she was in labor for 36 hours. I don't even want to do anything that feels GOOD for 36 hours.

Rita Rudner
(1956-) Comedian

I realize why women die in childbirth—it's preferable.

Sherry Glaser
Comedian, Activist

PREGNANCY

Insightful Observations on NATURAL CHILDBIRTH

HAVING BABIES

CHILDHOOD

TEENAGERS

PARENTING

HOME LIFE

RELATIVES

In the natural childbirth classes my wife and I took, the birthing process was represented by a hand puppet being pushed through a sock. So, at the actual birth, I was shocked to see all this blood. The thing I had prepared myself for was a lot of lint.

Steve Scrovan
Present Day Comedian

If you don't yell during labor, you're a fool. I screamed. Oh, how I screamed. And that was just during the conception.

Joan Rivers
(1933-) Actress, Comedian

What they put women through today when they're having a baby! They don't want to medicate them, as compared to previous generations. When my mom had me, she had so much medication, she didn't wake up till I was seven.

Dennis Wolfberg
(1946-1994) Actor, Comedian

I told my mother I was going to have a natural childbirth. She said to me, "Linda, you've been taking drugs all your life. Why stop now?"

Linda Maldonado
Present Day Journalist, Author

PREGNANCY

Insightful Observations on
FATHER PARTICIPATION

I like kids. They're fun to make.

Warren Ellis
Present Day Writer

That's how men participate now; they come into the room and say, "Breathe." Is that really sharing the experience? If I ever have a baby I want my husband to be on the table next to me, at least getting his legs waxed.

Rita Rudner
(1956-) Comedian

Try not to inspect your wife's episiotomy stitches. Sure, you'll get over it if you look, but if you're like me, you just don't need this in your memory bank.

James Douglas Barron
Present Day Relationship Expert, Author

You have this myth you're sharing the birth experience. Unless you're circumcising yourself with a chain saw, I don't think so. Unless you're opening an umbrella up your ass, I don't think so.

Robin Williams
(1952-) Comedian, Actor, Writer

I asked my husband if he wanted to be in the room with me when I gave birth. He said, "It would have to be a big room, and there would have to be a bar at one end."

Rita Rudner
(1956-) Comedian

To be a successful father there is one absolute rule: When you have a kid, don't look at it for the first two years.

Ernest Hemingway
(1899-1961) Author

28

BABIES

Insightful Observations on
THE NEW BABY

"I'm Ted. I'm 10 Months Old and I'm a Nudist."

 Julian Orenstein
Present Day Writer,
Columnist, Pediatrician

Every baby born into the world is a finer one than the last.

 Charles Dickens
(1812-1870) British Novelist

Life is truly a ride. We're all strapped in, and no one can stop it. When the doctor slaps your behind, he's ripping your ticket, and away you go. As you make each passage from youth to adulthood to maturity, sometimes you put your arms up and scream, sometimes you just hang on to that bar in front of you. But the ride is the thing. I think the most you can hope for at the end of life is that your hair's messed, you're out of breath, and you didn't throw up.

Jerry Seinfeld
(1954-) Comedian, Actor, Producer

In some cultures they don't name their babies right away. They wait and see how the child develops, like in Dances with Wolves. Unfortunately, our kids' names would be less romantic and poetic. "This is my oldest boy, Falls Off His Tricycle, his friend Dribbles His Juice, and my beautiful daughter, Allergic to Nuts."

 Paul Reiser
(1957-) Actor, Writer, Comedian

I'd hate to be a new baby being born into this world today. There seems to be so much trouble everywhere. If I were a new baby, I don't think I could stand knowing what I was going to have to go through. That's why they don't show them any newspapers for the first two years.

 Charles Schulz
(1922-2000) Cartoonist;
Peanuts

Having a baby is like suddenly getting the world's worst roommate, like having Janis Joplin (60's Rock Icon) with a bad hangover and PMS come stay with you.

 Anne Lamott
Present Day Writer

BABIES

Insightful Observations on
THE NEW PARENT

Having children gives your life purpose. Right now my purpose is to get some sleep.

Reno Goodale
Present Day Comedian

I remember leaving the hospital...thinking: "Wait, are they going to let me just walk off with him? I don't know beans about babies!"

Anne Tyler
(1941-) Novelist

You begin to understand paradox: lying on the bed next to him, you are deeply interested...and yet at the same time you are deeply bored.

Lydia Davis
Present Day Author

When you have a child, things are unscheduled chaos.

Wendy Shulman
Present Day Author

You never know what you're going to get, and children have their own personalities immediately. I was watching little kids on a carousel: Some kids were jumping on the horses, some kids were afraid of the horses, some kids were betting on the horses.

Rita Rudner
(1956-) Comedian

We have a new baby. It is composed of a bald head and a pair of lungs.

Eugene Field
(1850-1895) American Poet

HAVING BABIES · CHILDHOOD · TEENAGERS · PARENTING · HOME LIFE · RELATIVES

30

THE GUIDE TO LAUGHING AT FAMILY

BABIES

Insightful Observations on
THE NEW MOTHER

HAVING BABIES

CHILDHOOD

TEENAGERS

PARENTING

HOME LIFE

RELATIVES

I actually remember feeling delight, at two o'clock in the morning, when the new baby woke for his feed, because I so longed to have another look at him.

Margaret Drabble
(1935-) English Novelist

At the moment one's children are conceived, one ceases to be an ego and becomes merely a cosmic tube, a funnel into timelessness.

Erica Jong
(1942-) Writer, Poet

I am amazed (and secretly delighted) at how many people stop me to have a look at my baby. Motherhood seems to break all social barriers as conversations with strangers of all ages and backgrounds evolve.

Simone Bloom
Present Day Educator,
Author

You'll wake up some mornings and think, "How will I possibly get through this endless day within these four walls?"

The Riverside Mothers Group

Home alone with a wakeful newborn, I could shower so quickly that the mirror didn't fog and the backs of my knees stayed dry.

Marni Jackson
Present Day Journalist,
Best-selling Author

I think all my brain cells came out with the after birth!

Beth Wilson Saavedra
Present Day Author

New mom talking to female visitor on couch with baby clothes and bassinet: "I thought I liked babies, but, as it turned out, I mainly like baby clothes."

Barbara Smaller
Present Day Cartoonist in
The New Yorker

= IDEALIST = REALIST = CYNIC

31

BABIES

Insightful Observations on
THE NEW FATHER

I felt something impossible for me to explain in words. Then they took her away, it hit me. I got scared all over again and began to feel giddy. Then it came to me—I am a father.

Nat King Cole
(1917-1965) Singer,
Songwriter

When Charles first saw our child, Mary, he said all the proper things for a new father. He looked upon the poor little red thing and blurted, "She's more beautiful than the Brooklyn Bridge."

Helen Hayes
(1900-1993) Actress

Once you have a kid, you'll never win another argument with your wife. Because in the game of marriage, giving birth is a royal flush. Nothing trumps motherhood.

Reno Goodale
Present Day Comedian

To become a father is not hard. To be a father is, however.

Wilhelm Busch
(1832-1908), Poet, Painter,
Cartoonist

Men will now get up and walk with the baby in the middle of the night, change its diapers, and give it a bottle, but in their heart of hearts they still think they shouldn't have to.

Rita Rudner
(1956-) Comedian

I only have two rules for my newly born daughter: she will dress well and never have sex.

John Malkovich
(1953-) Actor

No one is more helpless than a newborn father.

Author Unknown

32

BABIES

Insightful Observations on
THE OLDER SIBLING

HAVING BABIES

CHILDHOOD

TEENAGERS

PARENTING

HOME LIFE

RELATIVES

My kid brother was sent from heaven. They must like it quiet up there.

 Author Unknown

My mom says I'm her sugarplum.
My mom says I'm her lamb.
My mom says I'm completely perfect
Just the way I am.
My mom says I'm a super-special wonderful terrific little guy.
My mom just had another baby.
Why?

 Judith Viorst
(1931-) Poet, Journalist,
Author

The question that's probably uppermost in the child's mind is: Why do my parents want to have a baby? Don't they love me? And if they love me, why do they need another one? Aren't I enough? Imagine for a minute yourself in a similar situation. Your husband comes home and says: "Honey I love you so much, I've decided to go get another wife so I can have two." How would you feel?

 Lawrence Balter
Present Day Psychologist,
Author; *Dr. Balter's Child
Sense*

A gorgeous example of denial is the story about the little girl who was notified that a baby brother or sister was on the way. She listened in thoughtful silence, then raised her gaze from her mother's belly to her eyes and said, "Yes, but who will be the new baby's mommy?"

 Judith Viorst
(1931-) Poet, Journalist,
Author

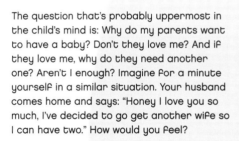

BABIES

Insightful Observations on
A BABY'S ROLE

CHILDHOOD

TEENAGERS

PARENTING

HOME LIFE

RELATIVES

Children reinvent your world for you.

 Susan Sarandon
(1946-) Actress, Political Activist

A baby is God's opinion that the world should go on.

 Carl Sandburg
(1878-1967) American Poet, Biographer

A baby is a blank cheque made payable to the human race.

 Barbara Christine Seifert
Present Day Writer

A baby will make love stronger, days shorter, nights longer, bankrolls smaller, homes happier, clothes shabbier, the past forgotten, and the future worth living for.

 Author Unknown

The guys who fear becoming fathers don't understand that fathering is not something perfect men do, but something that perfects the man. The end product of child raising is not the child but the parent.

 Frank Pittman
(1935-) Author

I don't know why they say "you have a baby." The baby has you.

 Gallagher
Present Day Comedian

One of the most obvious results of having a baby around the house is to turn two good people into complete idiots who probably wouldn't have been much worse than mere imbeciles without it.

 Georges Courteline
(1858-1929) French Novelist, Playwright

34

BABIES

Insightful Observations on
THE BABY'S PERSPECTIVE

Hi. I'm Bill. I'm a birth survivor.

Bill Maher
(1956-) Writer, TV Talk Show Host

Don't forget that compared to a grown-up person every baby is a genius. Think of the capacity to learn! The freshness, the temperament, the will of a baby a few months old.

May Sarton
(1912-1995) Belgian-American Poet, Novelist

Few things delight a baby more than her reflection.

Penny Warner
Present Day Writer, Columnist

The history of man for the nine months preceding his birth would, probably, be far more interesting and contain events of greater moment than all the three-score and ten years that follow it.

Samuel Taylor Coleridge
(1772-1834) British Poet

When I was a baby, I kept a diary. Recently I was re-reading it. It said: "Day One: Still tired from the move. Day Two: Everyone talks to me like I'm an idiot."

Steven Wright
(1955-) Actor, Writer, Comedian

When I was born, I was so surprised I couldn't talk for a year and a half.

Gracie Allen
(1902-1964) Comedian, Radio & TV Personality

BABY STEWIE: Do these Huggies make my ass look big?

Family Guy
Animated TV Show (1999-2002)

INSIGHTFUL OBSERVATIONS TO SHARE

35

HAVING BABIES

CHILDHOOD

TEENAGERS

PARENTING

HOME LIFE

RELATIVES

HAVING BABIES

CHILDHOOD

TEENAGERS

PARENTING

HOME LIFE

RELATIVES

BABIES

Insightful Observations on
UNDERSTANDING BABIES

What the mother sings to the cradle goes all the way to the grave.

 Henry Ward Beecher
(1813-1887) Clergyman, Abolitionist

Our attitude toward the newborn child should be one of reverence that a spiritual being has been confined within limits perceptible to us.

 Maria Montessori
(1870-1952) Physician, Educator

By the way, many people make the false assumption that because a baby can't speak, he can't hear. As a result, when confronted with an infant, any infant, they raise their voices and speak very distinctively, as though they were ordering a meal in a foreign language.

 Jean Kerr
(1922-2003) Writer, Dramatist, Lyricist

There is a great difference between knowing and understanding: you can know a lot about something and not really understand it.

 Charles F. Kettering
(1876-1958) Engineer Inventor

Do infants enjoy infancy as much as adults enjoy adultery?

 Author Unknown

If you were to open up a baby's head—and I am not for a moment suggesting that you should—you would find nothing but an enormous drool gland.

 Dave Barry
(1947-) Author, Humorist

A baby is an alimentary canal with a loud voice at one end and no responsibility at the other.

 Ronald Reagan
(1911-) 40th U.S. President, Movie Actor

36

BABIES

Insightful Observations on
CARING FOR BABIES

A baby is born with a need to be loved—and never outgrows it.

 Frank A. Clark
Present Day Author

Father reading parenting book, talking to wife holding a tiny baby: "According to this, everything we've done up to now is right."

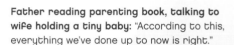 Edward Koren
Present Day Cartoonist in
The New Yorker

Babies don't need fathers, but mothers do. Someone who is taking care of a baby needs to be taken care of.

Amy Heckerling
(1954-) Writer, Film Director

Well, another year has gone by and still the Nobel Prize has not yet been awarded to the inventor of the Snugli baby carrier. I can't figure it.

Anna Quindlen
(1953-) Novelist, Social Critic, Columnist

The best thing is that baby intercom, so you can monitor your child. She's in her crib with her intercom, and can get me on mine, "Breaker One Nine, Dad. I've got spit-up on my shirt, and I'm packing a load. I could use some help out here."

Bob Saget
(1956-) Comedian, Actor, Director, Writer

Studies show rectal thermometers are still the best way to take a baby's temperature. Plus, it really shows them who's boss.

Tina Fey
(1970-) Comedian, Actress

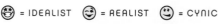 = IDEALIST   = REALIST   = CYNIC

37

BABIES

Insightful Observations on
CRYING BABIES

I just can't get over how much babies cry. I really had no idea what I was getting into. To tell you the truth, I thought it would be more like getting a cat.

Anne Lamott
Present Day Writer

My wife began to breast-feed our baby to relieve his ear pressure during takeoff. Which, I understand, hands down beats the hell out of chewing gum.

Paul Reiser
(1957-) Actor, Writer, Comedian

In came a baby, eloquent as infancy usually is, and like most youthful orators, more easily heard than understood.

L.E. Landon
(1802-1838) British Poet, Critic, Author

Getting down on all fours and imitating a rhinoceros stops babies from crying. (Put an empty cigarette pack on your nose for a horn and make loud "snort" noises.) I don't know why parents don't do this more often. Usually it makes the kid laugh. Sometimes it sends him into shock. Either way it quiets him down. If you're a parent, acting like a rhino has another advantage. Keep it up until the kid is a teenager and he definitely won't have his friends hanging around your house all the time.

P.J. O'Rourke
(1947-) US Humorist, Journalist, Political Commentator

This is the Basic Baby Mood Cycle:
Mood One: Just about to cry.
Mood Two: Crying.
Mood Three: Just finished crying.

Dave Barry
(1947-) Author, Humorist

I found out why God made babies cute. It's so you don't kill them.

Gallagher
Present Day Comedian

38

BABIES

Insightful Observations on
FEEDING BABIES

A child is fed with milk and praise.

Mary Lamb
(1765-1847) Writer, Poet

There are three reasons for breast-feeding: the milk is always at the right temperature; it comes in attractive containers; and the cat can't get it.

Irena Chalmers
Culinary author, Lecturer

A new father finds out the meaning of spitting image when he tries to feed cereal to his infant.

Imogene Fey
Present Day American Writer

A grandfather was taking a turn at feeding the baby some strained peas. Naturally, there were traces of the food everywhere, especially on the infant.

Author Unkown

His daughter comes in, looks at the infant, then at the old man staring into space and says, "What in the world are you doing?" He replied, "I'm waiting for the first coat to dry, so I can put on another."

Gary D. Christenson
Present Day Writer, Educator

One of the great ironies…is that feeding children, a task whose misery cannot be ignored, leads to more diaper changing. It actually says on the inside label of the Gerber food jar not to feed the kid out of the jar because it's unappetizing. Unappetizing? Have they seen that food? The strained green beans weren't exactly calling out to me to begin with!

Paula Poundstone
(1959-) Comedian, Writer, Actress

My mother didn't breast feed me. She said she liked me as a friend.

Rodney Dangerfeild
(1921-) Comedian, Actor, Writer, Producer

HAVING BABIES

CHILDHOOD

TEENAGERS

PARENTING

HOME LIFE

RELATIVES

HAVING BABIES

CHILDHOOD

TEENAGERS

PARENTING

HOME LIFE

RELATIVES

BABIES

Insightful Observations on
CHANGING DIAPERS

Just when you're getting bored with changing diapers, another surprise turns up in one.

 Arlene Eisenberg, Heidi E. Murkoff, and Sandee E. Hathaway
Present Day Authors; *What to Expect Book Series*

I hate changing my baby's diapers after he poops. I know exactly what he ate at day care. Yesterday, it was carrots. Tomorrow, I'm hoping for long-stemmed roses.

 Shirley Lipner
Present Day Comedian

One of the most important things to remember about infant care is: never change the diapers in mid-stream.

 Don Marquis
(1878-1937) Humorist, Author

How to fold a diaper depends on the size of the baby and the diaper.

 Dr. Benjamin Spock
(1903-1998) Pediatrician, Psychiatrist, Author

Spread the diaper in the position of the diamond with you at bat. Then fold second base down to home and set the baby on the pitcher's mound. Put first base and third together, bring up home plate and pin the three together. Of course, in case of rain, you gotta call the game and start all over again.

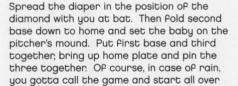 Jimmy Piersall
(1929-) Baseball Player; **on how to diaper a baby**

Changing a diaper is a lot like getting a present from your grandmother—you're not sure what you've got, but you're pretty sure you're not going to like it.

 Jeff Foxworthy
(1958-) U.S. Comedian, Actor

Diaper backwards spells repaid. Think about it.

 Marshall McLuhan
(1911-1980) Educator, Communications Theorist

40

BABIES

Insightful Observations on
SLEEPING

Seeing you sleeping peacefully on your back among your stuffed ducks, bears, and basset hounds would remind me that no matter how good the next day might be, certain moments were gone forever.

 Joan Baez
(1941-) Folk Singer, Songwriter

In an answer to "How are you sleeping?" at a press conference, after the US invaded Iraq
GEORGE BUSH: Like a baby!
COLIN POWELL: Like a baby. I wake up every few hours screaming.

 George W. Bush
(1946-) 43rd U.S. President
& Colin Powell (1937-)
Secretary of State

It is little wonder that the voices of experience tell you to sleep whenever you can. Take, borrow, or steal your sleep time from any activity that is not absolutely essential for you or the baby. The baby cannot thrive if you can't.

 Daniel N. Stern &
Nadia Bruschweiler
Present day Authors

I can't decide if I want a baby. And my friends who have kids don't make very good salesmen. They're like, "Oh, you learn all this great stuff, like how to survive on two hours' sleep." If I want to learn that, I'll just become a political prisoner or something.

 Cathryn Michon
Present Day Comedian, Writer, Actress

People who say they sleep like babies usually don't have them.

 Leo J. Burke
(1937-) Educator

Little children disturb your sleep, big ones your life.

 Yiddish Proverb

INSIGHTFUL OBSERVATIONS TO SHARE

HAVING BABIES

CHILDHOOD

TEENAGERS

PARENTING

HOME LIFE

RELATIVES

HAVING BABIES

CHILDHOOD

TEENAGERS

PARENTING

HOME LIFE

RELATIVES

BABIES

Insightful Observations on
UNDERSTANDING TODDLERS

The fundamental job of a toddler is to rule the universe.

 Lawrence Kutner, Ph.D
20th Century Psychologist, Author, Columnist, Professor

The truth is, no matter how trying they become, babies two and under don't have the ability to make moral choices, so they can't be "bad." That category only exists in the adult mind.

 Anne Cassidy
(1952-) Journalist, Author

The toddler craves independence, but fears desertion.

 Dorothy Corkille Briggs
20th Century Parent Educator, Author

Paradoxically, the toddler's "No" is also a preliminary to his saying yes. It is a sign that he is getting ready to convert his mother's restrictions and prohibitions into the rules for behavior that will belong to him.

 Louise J. Kaplan
Present Day Psychologist, Author: Oneness and Separateness: From Infant to Individual

Nothing brings out a toddler's devotion to a toy she has abandoned more quickly than another child playing with it.

 Robert Scotellaro
Present Day Author, Children's Poet

42

BABIES

Insightful Observations on
THE NEXT BABY

My mom used to say it doesn't matter how many kids you have... because one kid'll take up 100% of your time so more kids can't possibly take up more than 100% of your time.

 Karen Brown
Present Day Writer

Your daughter sleeps through the night, you've lost the weight you gained in pregnancy, and you and your husband have resumed your usual romantic relationship. So everything's perfect...except for the tiny voice in your head that keeps saying, "Time to have another baby."

Author Unknown

Let me join in the chorus of people who should be telling you, YOU CAN GET PREGNANT WHILE YOU ARE NURSING, AND YOU CAN GET PREGNANT EVEN IF YOU HAVEN'T HAD A PERIOD YET.

 Vicki Iovine
20th Century Best-Selling Author

Having one child makes you a parent; having two makes you a referee.

 David Frost
(1939-) Writer, TV Talk Show Host

The third baby is the easiest to have.

 Shirley Jackson
(1919-1965) Author

I refused to have more than 2 children after reading that every 3rd child born in the world was Chinese.

 Harry Magnie
(1919-) Humorist, Master Carpenter

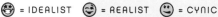 = IDEALIST = REALIST = CYNIC

HAVING BABIES

CHILDHOOD

TEENAGERS

PARENTING

HOME LIFE

RELATIVES

BABIES

Insightful Observations on
OTHER PEOPLES' BABIES

To me, they all look like Winston Churchill.

Shawn Thompson
(1967-) Writer, Film Director

My friends want to show me films of their baby's birth. No, thank you. But I'll look at a video of the conception if you've got one.

Garry Shandling
(1949-) Actor, Writer, Comedian

Ivy and Herbert have just had another baby, and they asked me to go along and see the little stranger. They asked me what I thought it was. I got it in three guesses. Herbert says it will be a member of Parliament when it grows up, because it can say so many things that sound good and mean nothing.

Jack Warner
(1896-1981) British Actor

Keep the poop talk to a minimum. While you might think your single childless friends are obligated to listen to your detailed descriptions of your infant's bowel movements just because you often listened to blow-by-blow accounts of their hapless love affairs, remember: sex is always more interesting than poop.

C.E. Crimmins
Present Day Author, Humorist

My sister is pregnant with her fifth baby and had the nerve to tell me she's registered at Babies "R" Us. No way. I'm drawing the line! Where's my gift for not getting knocked up? I made it my whole life so far without getting pregnant once. And that's a real accomplishment because I'm a slut.

Shelley Brigman
Present Day Comedian, Writer, Actress

44

Insightful Observations

Step Two:

CHILD

HOOD

Relating to Children
Raising Children
Types of Children
Teaching Lessons
Brothers & Sisters

HAVING BABIES

CHILDHOOD

TEENAGERS

PARENTING

HOME LIFE

RELATIVES

RELATING TO CHILDREN

Insightful Observations on
BEING A CHILD

A child is the greatest poem ever known.

 Christopher Morley
(1890 – 1957) Journalist, Author

If one is not going to take the necessary precautions to avoid having parents, one must undertake to bring them up.

 Quentin Crisp
(1908-1999) Actor, Writer, Model

You are worried about seeing him spend his early years in doing nothing. What! Is it nothing to be happy? Nothing to skip, play, and run around all day long? Never in his life will he be so busy again.

Jean-Jacques Rousseau
(1712-1778) French Philosopher, Author

The elders still say: "You know I have been young once, but you never have been old." But today's kids can replay: "You've never been young in the world I am young in, and you can never be."

Margaret Mead
(1901-1978) Anthropologist

Children are unpredictable. You never know what inconsistency they're going to catch you in next.

Franklin P. Jones
(1853-1935) Entertainer

A child is someone who stands halfway between an adult and a TV set.

 Author Unknown

What are kids, really, but little stupid people who live in your house and don't pay rent?

 Rick Reynolds
(1951-) Comedian, Writer

48

RELATING TO CHILDREN

Insightful Observations on
GETTING ALONG WITH CHILDREN

HAVING BABIES

CHILDHOOD

TEENAGERS

PARENTING

HOME LIFE

RELATIVES

My daughter, Lourdes, and I listen to Britney Spears songs together.

 Madonna
(1958-) Singer, Songwriter, Children's Book Author

Kids love to see me coming. Compared to most of the three-year-olds they know, I am a major slacker. My idea of an educational field trip is to pop them in the car and drive through the car wash screaming.

 Kate Clinton
(1945-) Comedian, Writer

Kids are at my level. I like goofing around with them.

 John Goodman
(1952-) Actor, Producer

To bring up a child in the way he should go, travel that way yourself once in a while.

 Josh Billings
(1818-1885) Humorist

One of the things I've discovered, in general, about raising kids is that they really don't give a damn if you walked five miles to school. They want to deal with what's happening now.

 Patty Duke
(1946-) Actress, Writer, Producer

Never play peek-a-boo with a child on a long plane trip. There's no end to the game. Finally I grabbed him by the bib and said, "Look, it's always gonna be me!"

 Rita Rudner
(1956-) Comedian

My children weary me. I can only see them as defective adults; feckless, destructive, frivolous, sensual, humorless.

 Evelyn Waugh
(1903-1966) British Novelist

 = IDEALIST   = REALIST   = CYNIC

49

HAVING BABIES

CHILDHOOD

TEENAGERS

PARENTING

HOME LIFE

RELATIVES

RELATING TO CHILDREN

Insightful Observations on
CHILDHOOD PROBLEMS

The hardest part about being a kid is knowing you have got your whole life ahead of you.

 Jane Wagner
(1935-) Writer, Director

We should not make light of the troubles of children. They are worse than ours, because we can see the end of our trouble and they can never see any end.

 William Middleton
Present Day Author

A door is something you're on the wrong side of when you're too short to reach the knob. When you are tall enough to reach the knob, a door is something you have left open if it's supposed to be closed, or closed if it's supposed to be open. You can't win.

 Robert Paul Smith
(1915-) American Author

Whichever you do, you have done it wrong. So close all open doors and open all closed doors. You will still be wrong, but you will be busy.

 Alec Wilkinson
Present Day Author, Journalist

A child is a territory, a landscape, a region, an outpost, a republic, an island of worry.

 Jerry Seinfeld
(1954-) Comedian, Actor, Producer

The only memory I have of being a Cub Scout was trying to get my hat back. That was all I did. Run back and forth at my bus stop going, "Quit it!"

 Kingsley Amis
(1922-1995) British novelist

It was no wonder that people were so horrible when they started life as children. Youth is a malady of which one becomes cured a little every day.

Benito Mussolini
(1883-1945) Italian Dictator;
said on his 50th birthday

50

RELATING TO CHILDREN

Insightful Observations on MANAGING CHILDREN

HAVING BABIES

CHILDHOOD

TEENAGERS

PARENTING

HOME LIFE

RELATIVES

You can do anything with children if you only play with them.

😵 **Bismarck**
(1815-1898) German Statesman

That energy which makes a child hard to manage is the energy which afterward makes him a manager of life.

😵 **Henry Ward Beecher**
(1813-1887) Clergyman, Abolitionist

Oh, what a tangled web do parents weave, when they think that their children are naïve.

😊 **Ogden Nash**
(1902-1971) Poet, Humorist

Everyone is in awe of the lion tamer in a cage with half a dozen lions—everyone but a school bus driver.

😊 **Author Unknown**

The quickest way for a parent to get a child's attention is to sit down and look comfortable.

😊 **Lane Olinghouse**
20th Century Writer

Mothers have to remember what food each child likes or dislikes, which one is allergic to penicillin and hamster fur, who gets carsick and who isn't kidding when he stands outside the bathroom door and tells you what's going to happen if he doesn't get in right away. It's tough. If they all have the same hair color they tend to run together.

😊 **Erma Bombeck**
(1927-1996) Humorist, Author

Mothers mold the children's minds. Some of you have done well. There are a lot of moldy-minded kids around.

😊 **Norm Crosby**
(1927-) Comedian, Actor

WELLNESS THROUGH LAUGHTER

HAVING BABIES

CHILDHOOD

TEENAGERS

PARENTING

HOME LIFE

RELATIVES

RELATING TO CHILDREN

Insightful Observations on
UNDERSTANDING CHILDREN

It takes practice for adults to change over every so often to Children's Standard Time.

 Fred Rogers
(1928-2003) Creator & Host of TV Show; *Mister Roger's Neighborhood*

Childhood is measured out by sounds and smells and sights, before the dark hour of reason grows.

 John Betjeman
(1906-1984) British Poet Laureate

Children don't walk like other people...they canter, they bounce, they slither, slide, crawl, leap into the air, saunter, stand on their heads, swing from branch to branch...or trot like ostriches. But I seldom recall seeing a child just plain walk. They can, however, dawdle.

 Phyllis McGinley
(1905-1978) Author, Poet

Children's talent to endure stems from their ignorance of alternatives.

 Maya Angelou
(1928-) Author

The business of being a child interests a child not at all. Children very rarely play at being other children.

 David Holloway
(1924-) Literary Editor

Children are different—mentally, physically, spiritually, quantitatively, qualitatively; and furthermore, they're all a bit nuts.

 Jean Kerr
(1922-2003) Writer, Dramatist, Lyricist

A child is a curly, dimpled lunatic.

 Ralph Waldo Emerson
(1803-1882) Author, Poet, Philosopher

RELATING TO CHILDREN

Insightful Observations on
UNDERSTANDING BOYS

HAVING BABIES

CHILDHOOD

TEENAGERS

PARENTING

HOME LIFE

RELATIVES

A man loves his sweetheart the most, his wife the best, but his mother the longest.

Irish Proverb

When a boy is growing, he has a wolf in his belly.

German Proverb

I know a little boy who told me...he could have easily won the race at his school except there was another boy who ran faster.

Stephen Leacock
(1869-1944) British-Canadian Author, Educator, Economist, Humorist

Boys will be boys—and so will a lot of middle-aged men.

Kin Hubbard
(1868-1930) Journalist, Humorist

Boys are beyond the range of anybody's sure understanding, at least when they are between the ages of eighteen months and ninety years.

James Thurber
(1894-1961) American Cartoonist, Author

Boy, *n*.: a noise with dirt on it

Not Your Average Dictionary

HAVING BABIES

CHILDHOOD

TEENAGERS

PARENTING

HOME LIFE

RELATIVES

RELATING TO CHILDREN

Insightful Observations on
UNDERSTANDING GIRLS

Say the word "daughter" slowly…notice the way it lingers on the tongue like a piece of candy.

😎 **Paul Engle**
(1908-1991) Poet, Novelist, Playwright

A girl is Innocence playing in the mud, Beauty standing on it's head, and Motherhood dragging a doll by the foot.

😎 **Alan Beck**
20th Century Writer; *What Is A Little Girl?*

Three little maids from school are we,
Pert as a school-girl well can be,
Filled to the brim with girlish glee.

😎 **W. S. Gilbert**
(1836-1911) British Dramatist

A little girl was arriving late from school, so the mother asked her why: "I had to help another girl. She was in trouble," replied the daughter. "What did you do to help her?" "Oh, I sat down and helped her cry."

😎 **Author Unknown**

She's stubborn, contrary, and willful.
She'll grumble; she'll whine, and complain.
Her habits are terribly awfully smug.
Her actions are far from humane.
She's selfishly stingy and rotten.
She's lazily sluggish and slow.
Her manners are cleverly cunningly coy …
but…
No sweeter daughter I know.

😎 **Babs Bell Hajdusiewicz**
(1944-) Children's Author, Poet, Educator

I was never a child. I was always a menopausal woman in a child's body.

🙂 **Tracey Ullman**
(1959-) Actress, Singer

RELATING TO CHILDREN

Insightful Observations on
CHILD'S POINT OF VIEW

HAVING BABIES

CHILDHOOD

TEENAGERS

PARENTING

HOME LIFE

RELATIVES

There are no seven wonders of the world in the eyes of a child. There are seven million.

 Walt Streightiff
20th Century Writer

Kids could always resolve any dispute by calling it. One of them will say, "I got the front seat. I called it." And the other kid has no recourse. If there was a kid court of law, it holds up. "Your Honor, my client asked for the front seat." The judge asks, "Did he call it?" "Well, no." He bangs the gavel. "Objection overruled. He has to call it. Case closed."

 Jerry Seinfeld
(1954-) Comedian, Actor,
Producer

One of the most obvious facts about grown-ups to a child is that they have forgotten what it is like to be a child.

 Randall Jarrell
(1914-1965) Author

Part of the reason for the ugliness of adults, in a child's eyes, is that the child is usually looking upwards, and few faces are at their best when seen from below.

 George Orwell
(1903-1950) British Novelist

To children, childhood holds no possible advantage.

 Kathleen Norris
(1880-1960) Author

Adults are obsolete children.

 Dr. Seuss
(1904-1991) Children's Author,
Cartoonist

 = IDEALIST   = REALIST   = CYNIC

55

RELATING TO CHILDREN

Insightful Observations on
STAGES OF DEVELOPMENT

The two-year-old—loves deeply, tenderly, extravagantly and he holds the love of his parents more dearly than anything in the world.

Selma H. Fraiberg
(1918-1981) Child
Psychoanalyst, Author

A three-year-old child is a being who gets almost as much fun out of a fifty-six dollar set of swings as it does out of finding a small green worm.

Bill Vaughan
(1915-1977) Journalist,
Author

The prime purpose of being four is to enjoy being four—of secondary importance is to prepare for being five.

Jim Trelease
Present Day Author;
Speaker; *The Read-Aloud Handbook* (1985)

I see the mind of a five-year-old as a volcano with two vents: destructiveness and creativeness.

Sylvia Ashton-Warner
(1908-1984) Educator, Novelist

Life begins at six—at least in the minds of six-year-olds... In kindergarten you are the baby. In first grade you put down the baby...every first grader knows in some osmotic way that this is real life... First grade is the first step on the way to a place in the grown-up world.

Stella Chess
(1914-) Psychiatrist,
Professor of Child
Psychiatry, Author

When you are eight years old, nothing is any of your business.

Lenny Bruce
(1925-1966) Satirist,
Comedian

RELATING TO CHILDREN

Insightful Observations on CHILDREN AT PLAY

The playing adult steps sideward into another reality; the playing child advances forward to new stages of mastery.

 Erik H. Erikson
(1902-1994) Psychoanalyst, Author; *Childhood and Society*

Water fascinates kids. They run toward it, and they run away from it. They love it in a lake or an ocean, but it's a necessary evil in the bathtub. They'll swim in it, sail on it, dangle feet in it—but fight to keep it away from that sacred area behind the ears.

Art Linkletter
(1912-) TV Personality, Actor; Producer

…Playing comes from a deep sense of well-being that is the direct result of feeling in control of things, in contrast to the rest of his life, which is managed by his parents or other adults.

Bruno Bettelheim
(1903-1990) Psychologist

Girls… were allowed to play in the house… and boys were sent outdoors… Boys ran around in the yard with toy guns going kksshh-kksshh, fighting wars for made-up reasons and arguing about who was dead, while girls stayed inside and played with dolls, creating complex family groups and learning how to solve problems through negotiation and role-playing. Which gender is better equipped, on the whole, to live an adult life, would you guess?

Garrison Keillor
(1942-) Radio Host, Writer

HAVING BABIES

CHILDHOOD

TEENAGERS

PARENTING

HOME LIFE

RELATIVES

HAVING BABIES

CHILDHOOD

TEENAGERS

PARENTING

HOME LIFE

RELATIVES

RELATING TO CHILDREN

Insightful Observations on
IMAGINATION

Imagination is more important than knowledge.

 Albert Einstein
(1879-1955) Physicist

...to master reality by experiment and planning.

 Erik H. Erikson
(1902-1994) Psychoanalyst, Author

The best toy is one the child creates. Take your child outside and show him how to build forts out of sticks, make boats out of paper—the possibilities are infinite.

 Author Unknown

WILLY WONKA: There is no life I know to compare with pure imagination. Living there, you'll be free if you truly wish to be.

 Gene Wilder
in *Willy Wonka & The Chocolate Factory* (1971) written by Roald Dahl

No one shows a child the sky.

 African Proverb

Every time a child says, "I don't believe in fairies," there's a little fairy somewhere that falls down dead.

 J.M. Barrie
(1860-1937) British Author; *Peter Pan*

MEATWAD: I don't have any real dolls, I prefer to use my infinite imagination… cause I ain't got no damn money.

 Aqua Teen Hunger Force
Animated TV Show (2000) written by Matt Maiellaro & Dave Willis

58

RELATING TO CHILDREN

Insightful Observations on
COMMUNICATING WITH CHILDREN

HAVING BABIES

CHILDHOOD

TEENAGERS

PARENTING

HOME LIFE

RELATIVES

Yearn to understand first and to be understood second.

Beca Lewis Allen
20th Century Writer

Dad, if you really want to know what happened in school, then you've got to know exactly who's in the class, who rides the bus, what project they're working on in science, and how your child felt that morning... Without these facts at your fingertips, all you can really think to say is "So how was school today?" And you've got to be prepared for the inevitable answer – "Fine." Which will probably leave you wishing that you'd never asked.

Ron Taffel
Present Day Psychologist,
Author; *Why Parents
Disagree*

Notoriously insensitive to subtle shifts in mood, children will persist in discussing the color of a recently sighted cement-mixer long after one's own interest in the topic has waned.

Fran Lebowitz
(1950-) Writer; Humorist

A 4-year-old son was eating an apple in the back seat of the car, when he asked, "Daddy, why is my apple turning brown?"—"Because," his dad explained, "after you ate the skin off, the meat of the apple came into contact with the air, which caused it to oxidize, thus changing the molecular structure and turning it into a different color."—There was a long silence. Then the boy asked, "Daddy, are you talking to me?"

Author Unknown

The real menace in dealing with a five-year-old is that in no time at all you begin to sound like a five-year-old.

Jean Kerr
(1922-2003) Writer;
Dramatist, Lyricist

HAVING BABIES

CHILDHOOD

TEENAGERS

PARENTING

HOME LIFE

RELATIVES

RELATING TO CHILDREN

Insightful Observations on ADULT CHILDREN

I have these slumber parties with my father (Aerosmith's Steve Tyler), and when we can't sleep, We stay up all night trading beauty tips. He knows all about the good creams and masks.

 Liv Tyler
(1977-) Actress

We just call each other on the phone and whine about how we don't have time to get together.

Cathy Guisewite
(1950-) Cartoonist; Cathy

I went home for the holidays, and all the men in my family are bald, and all the women are fat. It's like a Metallica concert going on in my own home.

Dave Attell
(1965-) Actor; Writer

It takes a woman twenty years to make a man of her son, and another woman twenty minutes to make a fool of him.

Helen Rowland
(1876-1958) Novelist, Playwright

One mother can take care of ten children, but ten children can't take care of one mother.

Author Unknown

Children begin by loving their parents. After a time they judge them. Rarely, if ever, do they forgive them.

Oscar Wilde
(1854-1900) Poet, Playwright, Novelist

Adults are just kids who owe money.

T-Shirt Slogan

RELATING TO CHILDREN

Insightful Observations on
PARENT & CHILD NEGOTIATION

HAVING BABIES

CHILDHOOD

TEENAGERS

PARENTING

HOME LIFE

RELATIVES

When you are dealing with a child, keep your wits about you and sit on the floor.

 Austin O'Malley
(1858-1932) Writer;
Keystones of Thought

Whining is like chalk scratching on a blackboard for most parents.

 Nancy Samalin
Present Day Educator,
Author

The best way to get a puppy is to beg for a baby brother—and they'll settle for a puppy every time.

 Winston Pendelton
(1910-2001) Author, Humorist

It was like dealing with Dad—all give and no take.

 John F. Kennedy
(1917-1963) 35th U.S.
President; **after meeting
with Khrushchev**

A mere parent pitted against a child in a test of wills in a toy store is a terrible spectacle.

 George Will
(1941-) Political Syndicated
Columnist, TV Journalist

Reasoning with a two-year-old is about as productive as changing seats on the Titanic.

 Robert Scotellaro
Children's Book Author,
Illustrator

Children don't ask for things they don't want. They just don't want them after they get them.

 Howard Stevens
Present Day Author

 = IDEALIST   = REALIST   = CYNIC

61

RAISING CHILDREN

Insightful Observations on
KIDS TODAY

HAVING BABIES

CHILDHOOD

TEENAGERS

PARENTING

HOME LIFE

RELATIVES

Before you judge the younger generation remember who raised them.

 Author Unknown

These kids are gonna grow up without all the video games we had, like Pac-Man. We're gonna look even dumber trying to explain these games to kids when we're fifty: "When I was your age we had a yellow circle." "Oh my!" "And it ate fruit and got chased by ghosts." "Oh dear!"

 Nick Swardson
(1977-) Comedian, Actor, Writer

For the very first time the young are seeing history being made before it is censored by their elders.

 Dame Rebecca West
(1892-1983) British Writer

A "snapshot" feature in USA Today listed the five greatest concerns parents and teachers had about children in the '50s: talking out of turn, chewing gum in class, doing homework, stepping out of line, cleaning their rooms. Then it listed the five top concerns of parents today: drug addiction, teenage pregnancy, suicide and homicide, gang violence, anorexia and bulimia. We can also add AIDS, poverty, and homelessness… Between my own childhood and the advent of my motherhood—one short generation—the culture had gone completely mad.

 Mary Kay Blakeley
Present Day Journalist, Author

Children nowadays are tyrants. They contradict their parents, gobble their food, and tyrannize their teachers.

 Socrates
(469-399BC) Greek Philosopher

62

RAISING CHILDREN

Insightful Observations on
BRINGING UP CHILDREN

HAVING BABIES

CHILDHOOD

TEENAGERS

PARENTING

HOME LIFE

RELATIVES

How children survive being brought up amazes me.

 Malcolm Forbes
(1919-1990) Author, Publisher

The child supplies the power, but the parents have to do the steering.

 Dr. Benjamin Spock
(1903-1998) Pediatrician, Psychiatrist, Author

It is hard to raise sons; and much harder to raise daughters.

 Shalom Aleichem
(1859-1916) Yidish Writer

Raising children is a creative endeavor, an art, rather than a science.

 Bruno Bettelheim
(1903-1990) Psychologist.

Raising kids is part joy and part guerilla warfare.

 Ed Asner
(1929-) Actor, Producer

In spite of the six thousand manuals on child raising in the bookstores, child raising is still a dark continent and no one really knows anything. You just need a lot of love and luck—and, of course, courage.

 Bill Cosby
(1937-) Comedian, Actor

Before I got married, I had six theories about bringing up children. Now I have six children and no theories.

 John Wilmot
(1647-1680) Second Earl of Rochester

HAVING BABIES

CHILDHOOD

TEENAGERS

PARENTING

HOME LIFE

RELATIVES

RAISING CHILDREN

Insightful Observations on
RAISING BOYS

Boys do not grow up gradually. They move forward in spurts like the hands of clocks in railway stations.

Cyril Connolly
(1903-1974) British Journalist

The male is a domestic animal which, if treated with firmness and kindness, can be trained to do most things.

Jilly Cooper
20th Century Author

The computer is a great teaching tool for young people. For example, my home computer has an educational program that enables you to control an entire simulated planet—its ecology, its technology, its weather, etc. My ten-year-old son and his friends use this program a lot and we've all learned some important ecological lessons, the main one being: Never, ever put ten-year-old boys in charge of a planet. "Let's see what happens when you have volcanoes and nuclear war!"

Dave Barry
(1947-) Author, Humorist

The only time a woman really succeeds in changing a man is when he is a baby.

Natalie Wood
(1938-1981) Actress

Guys start out acting macho at an early age. Any parent will tell you that girl babies will generally display a wide-eyed curiosity about the world, whereas boy babies will generally try to destroy it.

Dave Barry
(1947-) Author, Humorist

Of all the animals, the boy is the most unmanageable.

Plato
(427-348 B.C.) Greek
Philosopher

64

RAISING CHILDREN

Insightful Observations on
RAISING GIRLS

HAVING BABIES

CHILDHOOD

TEENAGERS

PARENTING

HOME LIFE

RELATIVES

Thank heaven, for little girls
For little girls get bigger every day
Thank heaven for little girls
They grow up in the most delightful way!

Alan Jay Lerner
(1918-1986) Screenwriter,
Playwright, Lyricist

There are three books my daughter felt
were the most important influences in her
life: the Bible, her mother's cookbook, and
her father's checkbook.

Joyce Mattingly
Present Day Educator,
Writer

From birth to 18, a girl needs good parents,
from 18 to 35 she needs good looks, from 35
to 55 she needs a good personality, and
from 55 on she needs cash.

Sophie Tucker
(1884-1966) Singer,
Entertainer

Mothers need to have sharp eyes and
discreet tongues when they have girls to
manage.

Louisa May Alcott
(1838-1888) Author

It is only rarely that one can see in a little
boy the promise of a man, but one can
almost always see in a little girl the threat
of a woman.

Alexandre Dumas
(1802-1870) French
Playwright, Novelist

INSIGHTFUL OBSERVATIONS TO SHARE

HAVING BABIES

CHILDHOOD

TEENAGERS

PARENTING

HOME LIFE

RELATIVES

RAISING CHILDREN

Insightful Observations on
TIME SHARED

Your children need your presence more than your presents.

Rev. Jesse Jackson
(1941-) Civil Rights Activist,
Political Leader

Sing out loud in the car even, or especially, if it embarrasses your children.

Marilyn Penland

Kids spell love T-I-M-E.

John Crudele
Present Day Professional
Public Speaker on Youth

All children wear a sign: "I want to be important NOW." Many of our juvenile delinquency problems arise because nobody reads the sign.

Dan Pursuit
(1911-) Author

Children make the most desirable opponents in Scrabble because they are both easy to beat and fun to cheat.

Fran Lebowitz
(1950-) Writer, Humorist

Every minute with a child takes seven minutes off your life.

Barbara Kingsolver
(1955-) American Novelist

RAISING CHILDREN

Insightful Observations on
PATIENCE

Dear GOD, I pray for patience. And I want it right now.

 Oren Arnold
(1900-1980) Author

Children allowed to develop at their own speed will usually win the race of life.

 Fred G. Gosman
Present Day Author

Everything about a new family takes time.

 Judy Blume
(1938-) Author

Children always take the line of most persistence.

 Marcelene Cox
20th Century Writer,
Columnist

What it really means to be a parent is: you will spend an enormous portion of your time lurking outside public toilet stalls.

 Dave Barry
(1947-) Author, Humorist

Mothers are basically a patient lot. They have to be or they would devour their offspring early on, like guppies.

 Mary Daheim
Present Day Author

 = IDEALIST   = REALIST   = CYNIC

HAVING BABIES

CHILDHOOD

TEENAGERS

PARENTING

HOME LIFE

RELATIVES

HAVING BABIES

CHILDHOOD

TEENAGERS

PARENTING

HOME LIFE

RELATIVES

RAISING CHILDREN

Insightful Observations on
NUTRITION

Praise them a lot. They live on it like bread and butter.

Lavina Christensen Fugal
(1897-1969) America's Mother of the Year, 1955

Toddlers are more likely to eat healthy food if they find it on the floor.

Jan Blaustone
(1952-) Author, Public Speaker

Maybe you're one of those parents who think a child won't develop a taste for sweets if she never eats anything with sugar in it. This is your first baby, isn't it?

Bill Dodds
20th Century Children's Book Author

A food is not necessarily essential just because your child won't eat it.

Katherine Whitehorn
(1928-) British Columnist, Author

My life is filled with cereal.

Phyllis McGinley
(1905-1978) Author, Poet

I'd been giving my kids Flintstone vitamins, but then I realized that Fred and Barney weren't exactly the pictures of health.

Buzz Nutley
Present Day Comedian

Nowadays, a balanced diet is when every McNugget weighs the same!

Mad Magazine

68

RAISING CHILDREN

Insightful Observations on
EATING HABITS

HAVING BABIES

CHILDHOOD

TEENAGERS

PARENTING

HOME LIFE

RELATIVES

To encourage my little kid to eat I'd sometimes say: "Just pretend it's sand."

 Author Unknown

In general, my children refuse to eat anything that hasn't danced on television.

 Erma Bombeck
(1927-1996) Humorist, Author

If they like it, it serves four; otherwise, six.

 Elsie Zussman
20th Century Columnist,
Author

Kids are without a doubt the most suspicious diners in the world. Will eat mud (raw or baked), rocks, paste, crayons, ball-point pens, moving goldfish, cigarette butts, and cat food. Try to coax a little beef stew into their mouths and they look at you like a puppy when you stand over him with the Sunday paper rolled up.

 Erma Bombeck
(1927-1996) Humorist, Author

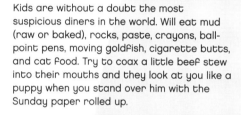

Spinach: divide into little piles. Rearrange into new piles. After five or six maneuvers, sit back and say you are full.

 Delia Ephron
Present Day Writer,
Producer

I do not like broccoli. And I haven't liked it since I was a little kid and my mother made me eat it. And I'm President of the United States and I'm not going to eat any more broccoli.

 George Bush
(1924-) 41st U.S. President

After Lois tries to feed Baby Stewie his broccoli "airplane style": "Damn you, Damn the Broccoli, and Damn the Wright Brothers!"

 Family Guy
Animated TV Show (1999-
2002)

HAVING BABIES

CHILDHOOD

TEENAGERS

PARENTING

HOME LIFE

RELATIVES

RAISING CHILDREN

Insightful Observations on
BEDTIME

The only thing worth stealing is a kiss from a sleeping child.

Joe Houldsworth
20th Century Author

The joys of motherhood are never fully experienced until the children are in bed.

Author Unknown

The persons hardest to convince they're at retirement age are children at bedtime.

Shannon Fife
(1888-1972) Writer

If anything makes a child thirstier than going to bed, it's knowing that his parents have gone to bed too.

Author Unknown

Child, speaking to father, about his wanting to read her a bedtime story: "That's O.K., Dad. I think I'll go with the ambient waterfall sounds tonight."

Robert Weber
Present Day Cartoonist in
The New Yorker

Anyone who thinks the art of conversation is dead ought to tell a child to go to bed.

Robert Gallagher
(1920-) Actor

RAISING CHILDREN

Insightful Observations on
PROTECTING CHILDREN

HAVING BABIES

CHILDHOOD

TEENAGERS

PARENTING

HOME LIFE

RELATIVES

Every cub has its mother's teeth to protect it.

 Author Unknown

A mother is not a person to lean on, but a person to make leaning unnecessary.

 Dorothy Canfield Fisher
(1879-1958) Author, Essayist

Sweater, n.: garment worn by child when its mother is feeling chilly.

 Ambrose Bierce
(1842-1914) Author, Satirist

When I was a kid, I used to imagine animals running under my bed. I told my dad, and he solved the problem quickly. He cut off the legs of my bed.

 Lou Brock
(1939-) Baseball Hall of Fame Member

I know that I could really kill for my daughter. I know because I'm living for her, so I'm fierce when it comes down to it. And I feel the same about my husband and my family. I'm just fiercely protective. It's like, that's my lair and nobody messes with my lair.

 Whitney Houston
(1963-) Actress, Singer

When I'm driving here I see a sign that says, CAUTION: SMALL CHILDREN PLAYING, I slow down, and then it occurs to me: I'm not afraid of small children.

 Jonathan Katz
Present Day Comedian, Actor, Writer

By the third kid, you know, you let 'em juggle knives.

 Mary Steenburgen
in *Parenthood* (1989) written by Lowell Ganz & Babaloo Mandel

71

HAVING BABIES

CHILDHOOD

TEENAGERS

PARENTING

HOME LIFE

RELATIVES

RAISING CHILDREN

Insightful Observations on
OVER PROTECTING

At every step the child should be allowed to meet the real experiences of life; the thorns should never be plucked from his roses.

Ellen Key
(1849-1926) Swedish Critic, Author

A child should not be denied a balloon because an adult knows that sooner or later it will burst.

Marcelene Cox
20th Century Writer, Columnist

It is not a parent's job to protect their kids from life, but to prepare them for it.

Blake Segal
20th Century Author

A child who consistently hears "Don't," "Be Careful," "Stop," will eventually be overtaken by schoolmates, business associates and rival suitors.

Marcelene Cox
20th Century Writer, Columnist

My parents warned me never to open the cellar door or I would see things I shouldn't see. So one day when they were out I did open the cellar door and I did see things I shouldn't see—grass, flowers, the sun...

Emo Philips
Present Day Comedian

RAISING CHILDREN

Insightful Observations on
KIDS & THE MEDIA

HAVING BABIES

CHILDHOOD

TEENAGERS

PARENTING

HOME LIFE

RELATIVES

No matter what the critics say, it's hard to believe that a television program which keeps four children quiet for an hour can be all bad.

Beryl Pfizer
20th Century Journalist, Former "Today Girl"

With all of its bad influences, TV is not to be feared… It can be a fairly safe laboratory for confronting, seeing through, and thus being immunized against unhealthy values so as to be "in the world but not of it."

Polly Berrien Berends
Present Day Author

I'm a Native American, my father was an Oneida tribal chairman, and when I watched cowboy movies as a kid, I thought, "My dad could kick John Wayne's butt!"

Charlie Hill
(1951-) Comedian, Actor, Writer

Not too many years ago, a child's experience was limited by how far he or she could ride a bicycle or by the physical boundaries that parents set. Today…the real boundaries of a child's life are set more by the number of available cable channels and videotapes, by the simulated reality of videogames, by the number of megabytes of memory in the home computer. Now kids can go anywhere, as long as they stay inside the electronic bubble.

Richard Louv
Present Day Journalist, Author; *Childhood's Future*

If you read a lot of books you're considered well-read. But if you watch a lot of TV, you're not considered well-viewed.

Lily Tomlin
(1939-) Actress, Comedian

Ninety-eight percent of American homes have TV sets—which means the people in the other two percent of the households have to generate their own sex and violence.

Author Unknown

 = IDEALIST   = REALIST   = CYNIC

HAVING BABIES

CHILDHOOD

TEENAGERS

PARENTING

HOME LIFE

RELATIVES

RAISING CHILDREN

Insightful Observations on
BABYSITTERS

Few mistakes can be made by a mother-in-law who is willing to babysit.

Author Unkown

A babysitter is a teenager who comes in to act like an adult while the adults go out and act like teenagers.

Henry Marsh
(1954-) Olympic Athlete, Author, Motivational Speaker

When you're looking for a sitter for your baby, be warned: Everyone looks like a hired killer.

Vicki Iovine
20th Century Best-Selling Author

They say you should video-tape your baby-sitter, but I don't think you should involve your kid in a sting operation.

Dave Chappelle
(1973-) Comedian, Actor, Writer

We used to terrorize our babysitters when I was little, except for my grandfather because he used to read to us from his will.

Janine DiTullio
Present Day Comedian, Actress, Writer

When you're a parent, you're a prisoner of war. You can't go anywhere without paying someone to come and look after your kids. In the old days, babysitters were fifty cents an hour; they'd steamclean the carpet and detail your car. Now they've got their own union. I couldn't afford it, so I had my mother come over. The sitters called her a scab and beat her up on the front lawn.

Robert G. Lee
Present Day Comedian, Writer

You feel completely comfortable entrusting your baby to the grandparents for long periods of time, which is why most grandparents flee to Florida at the earliest opportunity.

Dave Barry
(1947-) Author, Humorist

74

TYPES OF CHILDREN

Insightful Observations on ANGRY CHILDREN

HAVING BABIES

CHILDHOOD

TEENAGERS

PARENTING

HOME LIFE

RELATIVES

If you have never been hated by your child you have never been a parent.

 Bette Davis
(1908-1989) Actress

A child who has never fantasized about having other parents is seriously lacking imagination.

 Fred G. Gosman
Present Day Author; *How to be a Happy Parent... In Spite of Your Children*

Remember, when they have a tantrum, don't have one of your own.

 Judith Kuriansky
Present Day Sexologist, Columnist, Author, Radio Personality

Too often we underestimate the power of a smile, a kind word, a listening ear, an honest compliment, or the smallest act of caring, all of which have the potential to turn a life around.

 Leo Buscaglia
(1924-1998) Author, Lecturer

As a little girl my temper often got out of bounds. But one day when I became angry at a friend over some trivial matter, my mother said to me, "Elizabeth, anyone who angers you conquers you."

 Elizabeth Kenney
20th Century Educator

A trick that everyone abhors
In little girls is slamming doors.

 Hilaire Belloc
(1870-1953) French-born British Poet

75

WELLNESS THROUGH LAUGHTER

HAVING BABIES

CHILDHOOD

TEENAGERS

PARENTING

HOME LIFE

RELATIVES

TYPES OF CHILDREN

Insightful Observations on
UNHAPPY CHILDREN

It's never too late for a happy childhood.

 Gloria Steinem
(1934-) Writer, Feminist,
Political Activist

I was a born pessimist. My first words were, "My bottle is half empty."

 Lucie Harmon
Present Day Comedian

My childhood was so bleak, I wanted to stick my head in my Easy Bake oven.

 Mary O'Halloran
Present Day Comedian,
Actor

I'm paranoid about everything. At birth, I turned around and looked over my shoulder as I came out of the womb. I thought maybe someone was following me.

 Author Unknown

I was kind of a negative child. As a little girl I moved all my stuff into the basement so I could be even closer to hell.

 Penelope Lombard
Present Day Comedian,
Actor

If you're deep enough into denial to actually think that you did have a happy childhood, then your shrink will tell you that you must be forgetting something.

 Dennis Miller
(1953-) Actor, Comedian

TYPES OF CHILDREN

Insightful Observations on CLEVER CHILDREN

HAVING BABIES

CHILDHOOD

TEENAGERS

PARENTING

HOME LIFE

RELATIVES

Alas! That such affected tricks
Should flourish in a child of six!

 Hilaire Belloc
(1870-1953) French Born
British Poet

I was so smart when I was in grade school.
My Mother used to keep me home a few
days a week. This gave the other kids a good
chance to catch up.

 Harry Magnie
(1919-) Humorist, Master
Carpenter

VANESSA: Rudy, what would you do in life if you
only had a fourth grade education?
RUDY: Teach third grade.

 Tempestt Bledsoe
and Keshia Knight
Pulliam
on *The Cosby Show* (1984-
1992)

Clever father, clever daughter; clever
mother, clever son.

 Russian proverb

I never met anyone who didn't have a very
smart child. What happens to these children,
you wonder, when they reach adulthood?

 Fran Lebowitz
(1950-) Writer, Humorist

A child prodigy is one with highly imaginative
parents.

 Author Unknown

It is a dull child that knows less than its
father.

 Author Unknown

How to Raise your I.Q. by Eating Gifted
Children.

 Lewis B. Frumkes
20th Century Humorist,
Author; title of book

INSIGHTFUL OBSERVATIONS TO SHARE

TYPES OF CHILDREN

Insightful Observations on
DEFIANT CHILDREN

Children aren't happy with nothing to ignore, And that's what parents were created for.

Ogden Nash
(1902-1971) Poet, Humorist

Children in a family are like flowers in a bouquet. There's always one determined to face in an opposite direction from the way the arranger desires.

Madeline Cox
Present Day Columnist

Who has not watched a mother stroke her child's cheek or kiss her child in a certain way and felt a nervous shudder at the possessive outrage done to a free solitary human soul?

John Cowper Powys
(1872-1963) British Writer, Poet

Don't worry that children never listen to you; worry that they are always watching you.

Robert Fulghum
(1937-) American Philosopher, Writer

I was so naïve as a kid I used to sneak behind the barn and do nothing.

Johnny Carson
(1925-) Comedian, Talk Show Host

My kids can be cranky and don't like to take baths. They're like little Europeans.

Brian Kiley
Present Day Comedian, Writer

There was a time when we expected nothing of our children but obedience, as opposed to the present, when we expect everything of them but obedience.

Anatole Broyard
(1920-1991) Writer, *New York Times* Editor, Critic

78

HAVING BABIES
CHILDHOOD
TEENAGERS
PARENTING
HOME LIFE
RELATIVES

TYPES OF CHILDREN

Insightful Observations on SPOILED CHILDREN

HAVING BABIES

CHILDHOOD

TEENAGERS

PARENTING

HOME LIFE

RELATIVES

Ellie asked for a Baby G watch a couple of years ago, when those were very big with kids. It was $95 and I thought that was extravagant for a second grader. But there were kids in her class who had three of them!

 Katie Couric
(1957-) Television Journalist; **on not spoiling her kids just because she has the money to do so**

How sharper than a serpent's tooth it is To have a thankless child.

 William Shakespeare
(1564-1616) British Playwright, Poet

When you give your children material things as replacements for love, you teach them that it is objects, not love, which brings them happiness.

Barbara De Angelis
Present Day Author; Psychologist

I was in McDonald's and I saw this kid take his Happy Meal toy and throw it on the ground. His mom said, "Hey, you play with that. There are children in China who are manufacturing those."

 Laura Silverman
Present Day Comedian, Actress

Every mother knows that her most spoiled child is her husband.

 Walter Winchell
(1897-1972) Actor, Writer

 = IDEALIST = REALIST = CYNIC

HAVING BABIES

CHILDHOOD

TEENAGERS

PARENTING

HOME LIFE

RELATIVES

TYPES OF CHILDREN

Insightful Observations on
EXCUSES, LYING & MISCHIEF

When I was younger, I could remember anything, whether it happened or not.

Mark Twain
(1835-1910) Writer, Humorist

Telling lies and showing off to get attention are the mistakes I made that I don't want my kids to make.

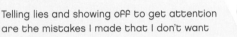
Jane Fonda
(1937-) Actress, Producer

The three-year-old who lies about taking a cookie isn't really a "liar" after all. He simply can't control his impulses. He then convinces himself of a new truth and, eager for your approval, reports the version that he knows will make you happy.

Cathy Rindne Tempelsman
Present Day Journalist, Author

The point is children lie to others for good and sufficient reasons, but they don't kid themselves. They know who did what, but they feel no moral imperative to inform grownups.

Leontine Young
20th Century Social Worker, Author

RAY BARONE: She had that look like Mom did when we were kids and she caught us eating that whole box of Sucrets, remember?
ROBERT BARONE: Yeah, my tongue was numb for a month.
RAY BARONE: Remember, Mom thought we were drug addicts. She said, "That's how it starts."

Ray Romano to Brad Garrett
in *Everybody Loves Raymond* TV Sitcom

TYPES OF CHILDREN

Insightful Observations on OUTSPOKEN CHILDREN

HAVING BABIES

CHILDHOOD

TEENAGERS

PARENTING

HOME LIFE

RELATIVES

Pretty much all the honest truth telling in the world is done by children.

Oliver Wendell Holmes
(1809-1894) Writer, Physician

Don't tell your two-year-old she's driving you nuts. She just might say, 'Mama nuts', to everyone she meets

Jan Blaustone
(1952-) Author, Public Speaker

The little girl had the making of a poet in her who, being told to be sure of her meaning before she spoke, said, "How can I know what I think till I see what I say?"

Graham Wallas
(1858-1932) English Political Scientist, Psychologist

First you have to teach a child to talk, then you have to teach it to be quiet.

Herbert Prochnow
20th Century Writer

There are only two things a child will share willingly—communicable diseases and his mother's age.

Dr. Benjamin Spock
(1903-1998) Pediatrician, Psychiatrist, Author

When you were a quiet little boy, somebody ought to have said, "hush" just once.

Mrs. Patrick Campbell to George Bernard Shaw
(1856-1950) Playwright

TYPES OF CHILDREN

Insightful Observations on
DESTRUCTIVE CHILDREN

An unbreakable toy is good for breaking other toys.

 Author Unknown

A truly appreciative child will break, lose, spoil, or fondle to death any really successful gift within a matter of minutes.

 Russell Lynes
(1910-1991) Writer, Editor

The surface of a table can be cluttered and breakable in the exact proportion to the age of the children who pass it by.

 Dorothy Evson
20th Century Educator, Author

Give a small boy a hammer and he will find everything he encounters needs pounding.

 Abraham Kaplan
(1931-) Orchestral Conductor, Composer

I like my kids a lot, but it's like a rodeo clown car pulled up and fifteen of them got out and they're running around. It's like they're monkeys on acid and they're hanging on lamps and lights and the ceiling. Get down!

 Denis Leary
(1957-) Comedian, Actor, Producer, Writer

TYPES OF CHILDREN

Insightful Observations on
CREATIVE CHILDREN

HAVING BABIES

CHILDHOOD

TEENAGERS

PARENTING

HOME LIFE

RELATIVES

A child's attitude toward everything is an artist's attitude.

 Willa Cather
(1873-1947) American Novelist

When I was in the second grade, we had to color the fruits their right colors, but I colored them all yellow. The teacher said, "Don't you know that an apple is red and an orange is orange?" I said, "Yes, but I like yellow."

 Goldie Hawn
(1945-1945) Actress

Kids: they dance before they learn there is anything that isn't music.

 William Stafford
(1914-1993) American Poet

It is not easy to be crafty and winsome at the same time, and few accomplish it after the age of six.

 John W. Gardner & Francesca Gardner Reese
Present Day Authors; *Quotations of Wit and Wisdom: Know or Listen to Those Who Know* (1996)

Every child is an artist. The problem is how to remain an artist once he grows up.

 Pablo Picasso
(1881-1973) Spanish Painter, Sculptor

My dad, he's a nuclear physicist, my mom, she's a mathematician, my brother is a chemical engineer – and I like to color.

 Shashi Bhatia
Present Day Comedian, Actor

I was a boring child. Whenever we played doctor, the other children always made me the anesthesiologist.

 Rita Rudner
(1956-) Comedian

83

INSIGHTFUL OBSERVATIONS TO SHARE

HAVING BABIES

CHILDHOOD

TEENAGERS

PARENTING

HOME LIFE

RELATIVES

TYPES OF CHILDREN

Insightful Observations on
MESSY CHILDREN

It will be gone before you know it. The fingerprints on the wall appear higher and higher. Then suddenly they disappear.

 Dorothy Evslin
20th Century Author

Even when freshly washed and relieved of all obvious confections, children tend to be sticky.

 Fran Lebowitz
(1950-) Writer, Humorist

Let your kids play in the mud. The mud will wash off, but the memories will last a lifetime.

 R.D. Ramsey
20th Century Author

Teach your children to brush their teeth, brush their hair and brush the dog, but not with the same brush. The dog resents it.

 Peggy Goldtrap
Present Day Comedian

...and while I want you to keep looking well, I think that if you spent a little more time picking up your clothes instead of leaving them on the floor, it wouldn't be necessary to have them pressed so often.

 Jospeph Kennedy
(1915-1944) **to his son John Kennedy** (1917-1963) 35th U.S. President

I have seen my kid struggle into the kitchen in the morning with outfits that need only one accessory: an empty gin bottle.

 Erma Bombeck
(1927-1996) Humorist, Author

The one thing children wear out faster than shoes is parents.

 John J. Plomp
20th Century Writer, Humorist

TYPES OF CHILDREN

Insightful Observations on LOUD CHILDREN

For children, is there any happiness which is not also noise?

 Frederick W. Faber
(1814-1863) Author, Speech Writer

The child enters your home and for the next twenty years makes so much noise you can hardly stand it. The child departs, leaving the house so silent you think you are going mad.

 John Andrew Holmes
Present Day Author

Mother scolds young boy on street: "Not so loud, sweetie. We're in Europe."

 Peter Steiner
Present Day Cartoonist in *The New Yorker*

When my kids become wild and unruly, I use a nice, safe playpen. When they're finished I climb out.

 Erma Bombeck
(1927-1996) Humorist, Author

Until I was thirteen, I thought my name was "shut up."

 Joe Namath
(1943-) American Football Champion

 = IDEALIST   = REALIST   = CYNIC

HAVING BABIES

CHILDHOOD

TEENAGERS

PARENTING

HOME LIFE

RELATIVES

TYPES OF CHILDREN

Insightful Observations on
BEAUTIFUL CHILDREN

There is only one pretty child in the world, and every mother has it.

 Chinese Proverb

I have good looking kids. Thank goodness my wife cheats on me.

 Rodney Dangerfield
(1921-) Actor, Comedian

"Is this kid beautiful or is this kid beautiful?" I always ask to hear the choices again because they sound so similar.

 Paul Reiser
(1957-) Actor, Writer, Comedian

Nature makes boys and girls lovely to look at so they can be tolerated until they acquire some sense.

 William Lyon Phelps
(1865-1943) Educator, Literary Critic, Author

Adorable children are generally considered to be property of the human race. Rude children belong to their mothers.

 Judith Martin
(1938-) Etiquette Authority; pen name "Miss Manners"

A soiled baby with a neglected nose cannot consciously be regarded as a thing of beauty.

 Mark Twain
(1835-1910) Writer, Humorist

TYPES OF CHILDREN

Insightful Observations on
NOT SO BEAUTIFUL CHILDREN

Every beetle is a gazelle in the eyes of its mother.

 Arab Proverb

I was teased because I had a really flat-looking nose and before I got braces my teeth used to stick out a bit.

Catherine Zeta-Jones
(1969-) Actress

No one ever told me I was pretty when I was a little girl. All little girls should be told they are pretty, even if they aren't.

Marilyn Monroe
(1926-1962) Actress

There is not one female comic who was beautiful as a little girl.

Joan Rivers
(1933-) Actress, Comedian

Growing up, I was the plain one. I had no style. I was the tough kid with the comb in the back pocket and the feathered hair.

Cameron Diaz
(1972-) Actress

All Gods' children are not beautiful. Most of God's children are, in fact, barely presentable.

Fran Lebowitz
(1950-) Writer, Humorist

I was so ugly when I was born, the doctor slapped my mother.

 Henny Youngman
(1906-1998) Comedian, Violinist

HAVING BABIES

CHILDHOOD

TEENAGERS

PARENTING

HOME LIFE

RELATIVES

HAVING BABIES

CHILDHOOD

TEENAGERS

PARENTING

HOME LIFE

RELATIVES

TEACHING LESSONS

Insightful Observations on LEARNING

Learning starts with a failure; the first failure is the beginning of education.

John Hersey
(1914-1993) Author

They say lottery money goes to building schools. I think that's ironic. After people get educated they won't play the lottery.

Charlie Viracola
Present Day Comedian

A child of one can be taught not to do certain things such as touch a hot stove, turn on the gas, pull lamps off their tables by their cords, or wake mommy before noon.

Joan Rivers
(1933-) Actress, Comedian

When the child is twelve, your wife buys her a splendidly silly article of clothing called a training bra. To train what? I never had a training jock. And believe me, when I played football, I could have used a training jock more than any twelve-year-old needs a training bra.

Bill Cosby
(1937-) Comedian, Actor

The child does not begin to fall until she becomes seriously interested in walking, until she actually begins learning. Falling is thus more an indication of learning than a sign of failure.

Polly Berrien
Berends
Present Day Author; *Whole Child/Whole Parent*

Each day of our lives we make deposits in the memory banks of our children.

Charles R. Swindoll
20th Century Christian Author

A child educated only at school is an uneducated child.

George Santayana
(1863-1952) Philosopher, Writer

88

TEACHING LESSONS

Insightful Observations on
POTTY TRAINING

The area [of toilet training] is one where a child really does possess the power to defy. Strong pressure leads to a powerful struggle. The issue then is not toilet training but who holds the reins – mother or child? And the child has most of the ammunition!

When we watched *Peter Pan*, my six-year-old came up with a beautiful question. "Daddy, how does Captain Hook wipe himself?

The baby is great. My wife and I have just started potty training. Which I think is important, because when we wanna potty-train the baby we should set an example.

There are hundreds of different toilet training methods—probably because none of them work.

PETER GRIFFIN: I'm looking for some toilet training books.
SALESMAN: We have the popular Everybody Poops, or the less popular Nobody Poops But You.
PETER GRIFFIN: Well, you see, we're Catholic…
SALESMAN: Ah, then you'll want You're A Naughty, Naughty Boy, And That's Concentrated Evil Coming Out The Back Of You.

☺ **Dorothy Corkille Briggs**
Present Day Parent
Educator, Author

☺ **Bob Saget**
(1956-) Comedian, Actor,
Director, Writer

☺ **Howie Mandel**
(1955-) Comedian, Actor,
Producer, Writer

☺ **Bruce Lansky**
Present Day Poet, Writer

☺ **Family Guy**
Animated TV Show (1999-2002)

INSIGHTFUL OBSERVATIONS TO SHARE

HAVING BABIES

CHILDHOOD

TEENAGERS

PARENTING

HOME LIFE

RELATIVES

TEACHING LESSONS

Insightful Observations on
RESPECT

If a mother respects both herself and her child from the first day onward, she will never have to teach respect.

Alice Miller
(1923-) Psychologist, Child Development Expert, Author; *The Drama of the Gifted Child*

During my second year of nursing school our professor gave us a quiz. I breezed through the questions until I read the last one: "What is the first name of the woman who cleans the school?" Surely this was a joke. I had seen the cleaning woman several times, but how would I know her name? I handed in my paper, leaving the last question blank. Before the class ended, one student asked if the last question would count toward our grade. "Absolutely," the professor said. "In your careers, you will meet many people. All are significant. They deserve your attention and care, even if all you do is smile and say hello." I've never forgotten that lesson. I also learned her name was Dorothy.

Joann C. Jones
20th Century Nurse, Author

There should be no forced respect for grown-ups. We cannot prevent our children from thinking us fools by merely forbidding them to utter their thoughts.

Bertrand Russell
(1872-1970) Philosopher, Mathematician

When I was a kid I got no respect. I told my mother, "I'm gonna run away from home." She said, "On your mark..."

Rodney Dangerfield
(1921-) Actor, Comedian

Never allow your child to call you by your first name. He hasn't known you long enough.

Fran Lebowitz
(1950-) Writer, Humorist

Oh to be half as wonderful as my child thought I was when he was small, and only half as stupid as my teenager now thinks I am.

Rebecca Richards
20th Century Educator, Author

90

TEACHING LESSONS

Insightful Observations on
QUESTIONS & ANSWERS

The important thing is not to stop questioning.

 Albert Einstein
(1879-1955) Physicist

A child can ask questions that a wise man cannot answer.

 Author Unknown

Children ask better questions than do adults. "May I have a cookie?" "Why is the sky blue?" and "What does a cow say?" are far more likely to elicit a cheerful response than "Where's your manuscript?" "Why haven't you called?" and "Who's your lawyer?"

 Fran Lebowitz
(1950-) Writer, Humorist

Answering questions can be a responsibility. Children think that parents have all the answers. In the words of one child, children are "whyers" and parents "becausers."

 Ruth Formanek
20th Century Psychologist, Educator, Author; *Why? Children's Questions*

What I learned is that if I don't know something, I just shrug my shoulders and admit it. Doctors don't know everything. Neither do teachers. Or dads.

 Frank McCourt
(1931-) Author

I grew up thinking my parents knew everything. I'm sure they didn't, but at least they were smart enough to fake it. I don't even know how to do that.

 Paul Reiser
(1957-) Actor, Writer, Comedian

 = IDEALIST   = REALIST   = CYNIC

HAVING BABIES

CHILDHOOD

TEENAGERS

PARENTING

HOME LIFE

RELATIVES

HAVING BABIES

CHILDHOOD

TEENAGERS

PARENTING

HOME LIFE

RELATIVES

TEACHING LESSONS

Insightful Observations on
GOOD MANNERS

If the only prayer you said in your whole life was, "thank you," that would suffice.

 Meister Eckhart
(1260-1328) German Mystic, Christian Theologian

Good manners will often take people where neither money nor education will take them.

 Fanny Jackson Coppin
(1835-1913) African American Civil Rights Leader

Manners are a sensitive awareness of the feelings of others. If you have that awareness, you have good manners, no matter which fork you use.

 Emily Post
(1872-1960) Etiquette Authority

We are born charming, fresh and spontaneous and must be civilized before we are fit to participate in society.

Judith Martin
(1938-) Etiquette Authority; pen name "Miss Manners"

Good breeding consists in concealing how much we think of ourselves and how little we think of other persons.

 Mark Twain
(1835-1910) Writer, Humorist

Politeness is organized indifference.

 Paul Valéry
(1871-1945) French Poet, Critic

Children are natural mimics: they act like their parents in spite of every attempt to teach them good manners.

Author Unknown

TEACHING LESSONS

Insightful Observations on BUILDING CONFIDENCE

HAVING BABIES

CHILDHOOD

TEENAGERS

PARENTING

HOME LIFE

RELATIVES

Excellence is not a skill. It is an attitude.

 Ralph Marston
Present Day Inspirational
Speaker

Look at little Johnny there,
Little Johnny Head-in-Air.

 Heinrich Hoffman
(1809-1874) German Writer

Perhaps a child who is fussed over gets a feeling of destiny; he thinks he is in the world for something important and it gives him drive and confidence.

 Dr. Benjamin Spock
(1903-1998) Pediatrician,
Psychiatrist, Author

My efforts to say nothing but positive things to my son have become desperate. "You're the best, smartest, cutest, friendliest baby, you're...telekinetic. You move objects with thought and start fires with your brain."

 Andy Dick
(1965-) Comedian, Actor,
Director, Writer

The one most important thing kids need to help them survive in this world is someone who is crazy about them.

 Urie Bronfenbrenner
(1917-) Russian Psychologist,
Author

A child can never be better than what his parents think of him.

 Marcelene Cox
20th Century Writer,
Columnist

It doesn't hurt to be optimistic. You can always cry later.

 Lucimar Santos de Lima
20th Century South
American Author

If you want your children to improve, let them overhear the nice things you say about them to others.

 Haim Ginott
(1922-1972) Israeli Child
Psychologist

HAVING BABIES

CHILDHOOD

TEENAGERS

PARENTING

HOME LIFE

RELATIVES

TEACHING LESSONS

Insightful Observations on MOTIVATING

My mother never gave up on me. I messed up in school so much they were sending me home, but my mother sent me right back.

Denzel Washington
(1954-) Actor

If you want children to keep their feet on the ground, put some responsibility on their shoulders.

Abigail Van Buren
(1918-) Advice Columnist;
Dear Abby

Sometimes the best helping hand you can give is a firm push.

Joann Thomas
20th Century Author

Encouraging a child means that one or more of the following critical life messages are coming through, either by word or by action: I believe in you, I trust you, I know you can handle this. You are listened to, you are cared for, you are very important to me.

Barbara Coloroso
Present Day Parent
Educator, Author

There are no shortcuts to any place worth going.

Beverly Sills
(1929-) Actress

Parents: A peculiar group who first try to get their children to walk and talk, and then try to get them to sit down and shut up.

Wagsters Dictionary of Humor & Wit

My son has taken up meditation, at least it's better than sitting around doing nothing.

Max Kaufman
Present Day Humorist

TEACHING LESSONS

Insightful Observations on DISCIPLINE

HAVING BABIES

CHILDHOOD

TEENAGERS

PARENTING

HOME LIFE

RELATIVES

When dealing with a two-year-old in the midst of a tantrum, fathers need to be particularly watchful about the tendency to need to feel victorious.

 Dr. Kyle Pruett
20th Century Psychiatrist, Child Development Expert

Who could have supposed that this childhood punishment, received at the age of eight at the hands of a woman of thirty, would determine my tastes and desires, my passions, my very self for the rest of my life.

Jean-Jacques Rousseau
(1712-1778) French Philosopher, Author

The first idea that the child must acquire, in order to be actively disciplined, is that of the difference between good and evil; and the task of the educator lies in seeing that the child does not confound good with immobility and evil with activity.

Maria Montessori
(1870-1952) Physician, Educator

Any child can tell you that the sole purpose of a middle name is so he can tell when he's in trouble.

 Dennis Fakes
20th Century Humorist

You know you've lost control when you're the one who goes to your room.

Babs Bell Hajdusiewicz
(1944-) Children's Author, Poet, Educator

HAVING BABIES

CHILDHOOD

TEENAGERS

PARENTING

HOME LIFE

RELATIVES

TEACHING LESSONS

Insightful Observations on PUNISHMENT

If I have to sit in the corner for sayin' it, at least you could tell me what it means!

Hank Ketcham
(1920-2001) Cartoonist;
Dennis the Menace

THEO: Hey dad. Am I really in that much trouble?
CLIFF: Let me tell you something. Your mother and I go into the kitchen. You can go out and get in MY car. You can drive BACKWARDS to Coney Island, run over the hot dog man and TWO stop signs and you won't be in any more trouble than you are in now."

Malcolm-Jamal Warner and Bill Cosby
on *The Cosby Show* (1984-1992)

Children need love, especially when they do not deserve it.

Harold Hulbert
20th Century Author

When you plant lettuce, if it does not grow well, you don't blame the lettuce. You look for reasons it is not doing well. It may need fertilizer, or more water, or less sun. You never blame the lettuce. Yet if we have problems with our friends or our family, we blame the other person. But if we know how to take care of them, they will grow well, like the lettuce. Blaming has no positive effect at all, nor does trying to persuade using reason and argument. That is my experience. If you understand, and you show that you understand, you can love, and the situation will change.

Thich Nhat Hahn
20th Century Vietnamese Buddhist Monk, Poet, Peace Activist

Mother to her small son who is pointing a toy ray gun at her: "If you're not a good boy, Santa will bring you only educational toys."

Barbara Smaller
Present Day Cartoonist in *The New Yorker*

If a child shows himself to be incorrigible, he should be decently and quietly beheaded at the age of twelve lest he grow to maturity, marry and perpetuate his kind.

Don Marquis
(1878-1937) Humorist, Author

96

TEACHING LESSONS

Insightful Observations on SPANKING

When my mom got really mad, she would say, "Your butt is my meat." Not a particularly attractive phrase. And I always wondered, now what wine goes with that?

 Paula Poundstone
(1959-) Comedian, Writer, Actress

The tired mother finds that spanking takes less time than reasoning and sooner penetrates the seat of the memory.

Will Durant
(1885-1981) Writer, Actor

I read one psychologist's theory that said, "Never strike a child in anger." When could I strike him? When he's kissing me on my birthday? When he's recuperating from the measles? Do I slap the Bible out of his hand on Sunday?

Erma Bombeck
(1927-1996) Humorist, Author

Never raise your hand to your kids. It leaves your groin unprotected.

Red Buttons
(1919-) Composer, Actor, Comedian, Author

Every child should have an occasional pat on the back as long as it's applied low enough and hard enough.

Bishop Fulton J. Sheen
(1895-1979) Thologean, TV Pesonality

Smack your child every day. If you don't know why—he does.

 Joey Adams
(1911-1999) Columnist, Actor, Personality

 = IDEALIST   = REALIST   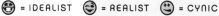 = CYNIC

TEACHING LESSONS

Insightful Observations on
GROWING OUT OF IT

My dad's probably one of the kindest people in the world. When I was younger that's not how I was—I was a little brat.

Leonardo DiCaprio
(1974-) Actor

Kids are cute, babies are cute, puppies are cute. The little things are cute. See, nature did this on purpose so that we would want to take care of our young. Made them cute. Tricked us. Then gradually they get older and older, until one day your mother sits you down and says, "You know, I think you're ugly enough to get your own apartment."

Cathy Ladman
(1955-) Comedian

Lawyers, I suppose, were children once.

Charles Lamb
(1775-1834) British Essayist, Poet

THE GUIDE TO LAUGHING AT FAMILY

TEACHING LESSONS

Insightful Observations on
BIRDS & THE BEES

The best sex education for kids is when Daddy pats Mommy on the fanny when he comes home from work.

Dr. William H. Masters
(1915-2001) Biologist, Sexual Therapist; Masters & Johnson Institute

Author Unknown

While I was visiting friends, the youngest member of the family, a seven-year-old boy, began to question his mother insistently about the facts of life. Patiently, she explained the miracle of life from conception, when large numbers of sperm raced towards the as yet unfertilized egg, through the nine months of pregnancy, to birth. As the lad sat quietly pondering over what he had heard, his expression changed gradually from puzzlement to understanding. Suddenly he grinned from ear to ear, leapt up, threw his arms around his mother, and cried, "And I won the race!"

One small girl to another as they sit reading a newspaper: "I think oral sex is when they only just talk about it."

Robert Weber
Present Day Cartoonist in *The New Yorker*

I was very sheltered growing up. I knew nothing about sex. My mother said this: "Sex is a dirty, disgusting thing you save for somebody you love.

Carol Henry
(1918-1987) Actor, Writer

HAVING BABIES

CHILDHOOD

TEENAGERS

PARENTING

HOME LIFE

RELATIVES

HAVING BABIES

CHILDHOOD

TEENAGERS

PARENTING

HOME LIFE

RELATIVES

TEACHING LESSONS

Insightful Observations on
READING

When you're a toddler, your favorite book isn't necessarily the one with the best story, or even the prettiest pictures. It's the one whose pages taste best. The book that goes easy on your gums is a great read. "I enjoy Faulkner's storytelling, but his novellas tend to cut me in the roof of the mouth. Dickens, on the other hand, soft and nice."

Paul Reiser
(1957-) Actor, Writer, Comedian

I've learned that when you read bedtime stories, kids really do notice if you use the same voice for the handsome prince that you used for the evil ogre the night before.

Author Unknown

As a child, my mother instilled in me a love of reading. In the eighth grade, I remember being home sick and reading Exodus by Leon Uris. She told me she was going to send a note to school saying I was home "sick in bed with Exodus."

Anne F. Ridgely
20th Century Author

Green Eggs and Ham was the story of my life. I wouldn't eat a thing when I was a kid, but Dr. Seuss inspired me to try cauliflower.

Jim Carrey
(1962-) Comedian, Actor, Writer

100

TEACHING LESSONS

Insightful Observations on
EDUCATION

HAVING BABIES

CHILDHOOD

TEENAGERS

PARENTING

HOME LIFE

RELATIVES

A good education is the next best thing to a pushy mother.

 Charles Schulz
(1922-2000) Cartoonist;
Peanuts

I keep six honest serving men, They taught me all I knew, Their names are What and Why and When, And How and Where and Who.

Rudyard Kipling
(1865-1936) English Writer;
Nobel Laureate

The whole purpose of education is to turn mirrors into windows.

Sydney J. Harris
(1917-1986) American
Journalist

If you are truly serious about preparing your child for the future, don't teach him to subtract—teach him to deduct.

Fran Lebowitz
(1950-) Writer; Humorist

If you think education is expensive, try ignorance.

Derek Bok
20th Century Lawyer;
Former University
President, Author

An education isn't how much you have committed to memory, or even how much you know. It's being able to differentiate between what you do know and what you don't.

Anatole France
(1844-1924) French Novelist,
Nobel Laureate

Mother talking to crying daughter: It's all right, sweetie. In the information age, everybody feels stupid.

 Peter Steiner
Present Day Cartoonist in
The New Yorker

INSIGHTFUL OBSERVATIONS TO SHARE

101

TEACHING LESSONS

Insightful Observations on
PRE-SCHOOL

My alphabet starts with this letter called yuzz. It's the letter I use to spell yuzz-a-ma-tuzz. You'll be sort of surprised what there is to be found once you go beyond 'Z' and start poking around!

 Dr. Seuss
(1904-1991) Children's Author, Cartoonist

Husband and wife interviewing for children's school: "We're looking for a preschool with an investment banking track."

 J.P. Rini
Present Day Cartoonist in *The New Yorker*

A kindergarten teacher is a woman who knows how to make things count.

 Author Unknown

If there were no schools to take the children away from home part of the time, the insane asylums would be filled with mothers.

 Author Unknown

Did you ever read that book, *Everything I Needed to Know I Learned in Kindergarten?* I learned only two things in kindergarten: First, if someone has something you want, you can remove it from them physically. And second, Elmer's glue makes a great between-meals snack.

 Gary Barkin
Present Day Humorist, Voice-Over Actor

I wasn't used to children and they were getting on my nerves. Worse, it appeared that I was a child, too. I hadn't known that before; I thought I was just short.

 Florence King
(1936-) Author; **on her first day of kindergarten**

102

TEACHING LESSONS

Insightful Observations on SCHOOLING

You send your child to the schoolmaster, but 'tis the schoolboys who educate him.

Ralph Waldo Emerson
(1803-1882) Author, Poet, Philosopher

Parents teach in the toughest school in the world: The School for Making People. You are the board of education, the principal, the classroom teacher, and the janitor, all rolled into two.

Virginia Satir
(1916-1988) Family Therapist, Author

It will be a great day when our schools get all the money we need and the air force has to hold a bake sale to buy a bomber.

Author Unknown

I have never let my schooling interfere with my education.

Mark Twain
(1835-1910) Writer, Humorist

Quite frankly, teachers are the only profession that teach our children.

Dan Quayle
(1947-) 44th U.S. Vice President

The regular course was Reeling and Writhing, of course, to begin with; and then the different branches of Arithmetic—Ambition, Distraction, Uglification, and Derision.

Lewis Carroll
(1832-1898) Victorian Author

A man who has never gone to school may steal from a freight car; but if he has a university education he may steal the whole railroad.

Franklin Delano Roosevelt
(1882-1945) 32nd U.S. President

 = IDEALIST   = REALIST   = CYNIC

103

HAVING BABIES

CHILDHOOD

TEENAGERS

PARENTING

HOME LIFE

RELATIVES

HAVING BABIES

CHILDHOOD

TEENAGERS

PARENTING

HOME LIFE

RELATIVES

TEACHING LESSONS

Insightful Observations on
TESTS & GRADES

Father reading a report card: One thing in your favor—with these grades, you couldn't possibly be cheating.

 Jacob Braude
20th Century Writer,
Humorist

You can get all A's and still flunk life.

 Walker Percy
(1916-1990) Writer

As long as there are tests, there will be prayer in schools.

 Author Unknown

Parents speak to child: Your mother and I have seen your report card, and we've decided to distance ourselves from you.

 Leo Cullum
Present Day Cartoonist in
The New Yorker

I was a total C student. If my son hands me his math homework, I'll have to say, "Hon, why don't you cheat off your little friends, or look it up in the back of the book like your father and I did.

 Janeane Garofalo
(1964-) Actress, Producer,
Comedian

Passing the SAT: My personal theory is that it has to do with how much money you send them in the mail. I think the amounts they tell you to send are actually just a suggested minimum donation—if you get my drift.

 Dave Barry
(1947-) Author, Humorist

BROTHERS & SISTERS

Insightful Observations on
LARGE FAMILIES

HAVING BABIES

CHILDHOOD

TEENAGERS

PARENTING

HOME LIFE

RELATIVES

I got more children than I can rightly take care of, but I ain't got more than I can love.

 Ossie Guffy
(1931-) Writer

Many people have said to me, "What a pity you had such a big family to raise. Think of the novels and the short stories and the poems you never had time to write because of that." And I looked at my children and I said, "These are my poems. These are my short stories."

 Olga Masters
(1920-1986) Australian Author

I came from a big family. As a matter of fact, I never got to sleep alone until I was married.

 Lewis Grizzard
(1947-) Southern Humorist

I grew up with six brothers. That's how I learned to dance—waiting for the bathroom.

 Bob Hope
(1903-2003) Comedian, Actor

I have five siblings, three sisters and two brothers. One night I was chatting with my Mom about how she had changed as a mother from the first child to the last. She told me she had mellowed a lot over the years: "When your oldest sister coughed or sneezed, I called the ambulance. When your youngest brother swallowed a dime, I just told him it was coming out of his allowance."

 Author Unkown

Lord have mercy, Mrs. Tugwell just had her sixteenth young'un. She had so many young'uns she'd run out of names—to call her husband.

 Minnie Pearl
(1913-1996) Comedian

The great advantage of living in a large family is that early lesson of life's essential unfairness.

 Nancy Mitford
(1904-1973) Writer

HAVING BABIES

CHILDHOOD

TEENAGERS

PARENTING

HOME LIFE

RELATIVES

BROTHERS & SISTERS

Insightful Observations on
BROTHERS & SISTERS

Behold how good and how pleasant it is for brothers and sisters to dwell together in unity.

 The Bible

A Sunday School teacher was discussing the Ten Commandments with her five and six-year olds. After explaining the commandment to "honor thy father and thy mother," she asked, "Is there a commandment that teaches us how to treat our brothers and sisters?" Without missing a beat, one boy (the oldest of a family of seven) answered, "Thou shalt not kill."

Author Unknown

Brothers and sisters are put on this earth to be teased and made to cry.

 Jenny Éclair
(1960-) Comedian, Writer

Of course, I could always depend on my brothers to tell me how bad I looked.

Dolly Parton
(1946-) Singer, SongWriter, Actress

Siblings: Children of the same parents, each of whom is perfectly normal until they get together.

 Sam Levenson
(1911-1980) Humorist, Author

BROTHERS & SISTERS

Insightful Observations on BROTHERS

HAVING BABIES

CHILDHOOD

TEENAGERS

PARENTING

HOME LIFE

RELATIVES

A brother is a friend provided by nature.

 Legouve Pere
20th Century French Author

The highlight of my childhood was making my brother laugh so hard that food came out of his nose.

 Garrison Keillor
(1942-) Radio Host, Writer

Brothers don't necessarily have to say anything to each other—they can sit in a room and be together and just be completely comfortable with each other.

 Leonardo DiCaprio
(1974-) Actor

When eight-year-old Joey's little sister underwent a necessary operation, it turned out she had lost so much blood she was in need of an immediate transfusion. Joey's blood was the same as his little sister's. "Will you give your sister some of your blood?" asked the doctor. Joey paused for a long time before he agreed. The boy tried to be brave as the blood was being drawn from his veins, but the doctor noticed he was growing paler and paler. When the draw was complete, Joey looked up at the doctor and timidly asked, "I was just wondering how long it will be before I die?" The doctor looked down at Joey and said, "Do you think people die when they give blood?" "Well, yes sir," replied Joey. "And you were willing to die for you sister?" "Yes sir," he said quietly.

 Author Unknown

My brother Russell, however, understood me well. He understood that I had great moves in bed, where the two of us constantly fought for control of one small mattress. Night after night in the darkness of our bedroom, we were opponents in pajamas. Although I was six years older than Russell, I managed to be just as immature.

 Bill Cosby
(1937-) Comedian, Actor, Producer

HAVING BABIES

CHILDHOOD

TEENAGERS

PARENTING

HOME LIFE

RELATIVES

BROTHERS & SISTERS

Insightful Observations on
OLDER BROTHERS

When you're a kid, it's so easy to have fun. What do you need? A book of matches, some oily rags, a little brother?

 Dave Attell
(1965-) Actor, Writer

My brother, Clyde, is a big old guy. When you open the dictionary to "cool," Clyde's picture is there. Clyde has his own theme music. When he walks down the street or into a room, you can hear him coming.

 Whoopi Goldberg
(1955-) Comedian, Actress, Producer

I have got a little brother two years old. I am eight. He always cries when you stick pins in him.

 Author Unknown

Older brothers invented terrorism. "Louie, see that swamp? There's a monster in it." So for years I walked way around it. Until I got a little older, a little wiser—and a little brother.

 Louie Anderson
(1953-) Comedian, Actor, Writer

Little Johnny went to the Doctor to get a vaccination. After the shot, the Doc pulled out a Band-Aid and started to cover the spot on his arm. Johnny asked him to put it on the other arm. "But if I put it over where you got the shot to let others know that it's tender and they shouldn't touch it," replied the Doc. Answered Johnny, "You really don't know much about little boys, do you ?"

 Author Unknown

108

BROTHERS & SISTERS

Insightful Observations on SISTERS

HAVING BABIES

CHILDHOOD

TEENAGERS

PARENTING

HOME LIFE

RELATIVES

Sisters have probably the most competitive relationship within the family, but once sisters are grown, it becomes the strongest relationship.

 Margaret Mead
(1901-1978) Anthropologist

A sister is a little bit of childhood that can never be lost.

 Marion C. Garretty
20th Century Author

Having a sister is like having a best friend you can't get rid of. You know whatever you do, they'll still be there.

 Amy Li
(1974-) Chinese Journalist

Sisters are always drying their hair. Locked into rooms, alone, they pose at the mirror, shoulders bare, trying this way and that their hair, or fly importunate down the stair to answer the telephone.

 Phyllis McGinley
(1905-1978) Author, Poet

She is your mirror, shining back at you with a world of possibilities. She is your witness, who sees you at your worst and best, and loves you anyway. She is your partner in crime, your midnight companion, someone who knows when you are smiling, even in the dark. She is your teacher, your defense attorney, your personal press agent, even your shrink. Some days, she's the reason you wish you were an only child.

 Barbara Alpert
Present Day Author

Life's a bitch, and life's got lots of SISTERS.

 Ross Presser
Present Day Humorist

109

 = IDEALIST = REALIST = CYNIC

HAVING BABIES

CHILDHOOD

TEENAGERS

PARENTING

HOME LIFE

RELATIVES

BROTHERS & SISTERS

Insightful Observations on
OLDER SISTERS

She was more like a magical older sister, my mother, in those impressionable days when the soft clay of my personality was being sculpted.

Gail Godwin
(1937-) Author; Short Story Writer

My sister taught me everything I need to know, and she was only in the sixth grade at the time.

Linda Sunshine
20th Century Writer, Editor

Look, take it for whatever it's worth, but my older sister swears she knows someone who's brother's friend disappeared up here a couple years ago during the summer.

Lindsey Leigh
in *Bloody Murder* (2000) written by John R. Stevenson

Mommy, Becky says she's not going to put me in her memoirs!

Liza Donnelly
Present Day Cartoonist in *The New Yorker*

Sis, I've been wondering...on my birthday mom always gives me five thousand dollars. How much does she give you?

Author Unknown

Big sisters are the crabgrass in the lawn of life.

Charles Schulz
(1922-2000) Cartoonist; *Peanuts*

110

BROTHERS & SISTERS

Insightful Observations on
SIBLING RIVALRY

HAVING BABIES

CHILDHOOD

TEENAGERS

PARENTING

HOME LIFE

RELATIVES

It goes without saying that you should never have more children than you have car windows.

Erma Bombeck
(1927-1996) Humorist, Author

Sibling rivalry is inevitable. The only sure way to avoid it is to have one child.

Nancy Samalin
Present Day Educator, Author

Two elderly sisters on a park bench wrapped up in winter coats and hats: "Am I the smart one and you're the pretty one or is it the other way around?"

Barbara Smaller
Present Day Cartoonist in *The New Yorker*

Last year, my father adopted one of those Save the Children, and now he compares me to his adopted child. "Why can't you be like your sister Kee Kee? Kee Kee dug an irrigation ditch for a whole village. What the hell are you doing with your life?"

Corey Kahane
(1963-) Actor, Comedian

It's a fact of life: Children will naturally seek to gain the upper hand in a family, often at the expense of a younger or more vulnerable sibling. They will observe one another closely and take advantage of any edge they can achieve.

Nancy Samalin
Present Day Educator, Author

It is true that I was born in Iowa, but I can't speak for my twin sister.

Abigail Van Buren
(1918-) Advice Columnist; *Dear Abby*, **Talking about her sister, Ann Landers**

Ask my brother (Harpo) how much he's made and that's how much I've lost.

Chico Marx
(1886-1961) part of Marx Brother's Comedy Team

HAVING BABIES

CHILDHOOD

TEENAGERS

PARENTING

HOME LIFE

RELATIVES

BROTHERS & SISTERS

Insightful Observations on
ONLY CHILDREN

Never fret for an only son. The idea of failure will never occur to him.

 George Bernard Shaw
(1856-1950) Playwright, Novelist, Critic

When you're the only pea in the pod, your parents are likely to get you confused with the Hope Diamond.

 Russell Baker
(1925-) Columnist, Humorist

I am married to Beatrice Salkeld, a painter. We have no children, except me.

 Brendan Behan
(1923-1964) Irish Playwright

They have big egos, a lot of them—if they are not crushed. You can think you are the center of the universe.

 Ruby Wax
(1953-) Actress, Comedian, Writer

I'm an only child, and it wasn't always easy. A lot of games were hard to play. Like catch. God, that was tiring.

 Dominic Dierkes
Present Day Comedian

When I was a girl I only had two friends, and they were imaginary. And they would only play with each other.

 Rita Rudner
(1956-) Comedian

We had a quicksand box in our backyard. I was an only child, eventually.

 Steven Wright
(1955-) Actor, Writer, Comedian

112

Insightful Observations

_____
_____
_____
_____
_____
_____
_____
_____
_____
_____
_____
_____
_____
_____
_____
_____
_____
_____
_____
_____

HAVING BABIES

CHILDHOOD

TEENAGERS

PARENTING

HOME LIFE

RELATIVES

INSIGHTFUL OBSERVATIONS TO SHARE

Step Three:

TEEN

AGERS

Relating to Teens

Social Life

Teen Dating

Leaving Home

RELATING TO TEENS

Insightful Observations on
UNDERSTANDING TEENS

HAVING BABIES

CHILDHOOD

TEENAGERS

PARENTING

HOME LIFE

RELATIVES

A normal adolescent isn't a normal adolescent if he acts normal.

 Judith Viorst
(1931-) Poet, Journalist, Author

If you truly want to understand something, try to change it.

 Kurt Lewin
(1890-1947) Psychological Theorist

Children from ten to twenty don't want to be understood. Their whole ambition is to feel strange and alien and misinterpreted so they can live austerely in some tower of adolescence, their privacies unviolated.

 Phyllis McGinley
(1905-1978) Author, Poet

Adolescence involves our nutty-desperate-ecstatic-rash psychological efforts to come to terms with new bodies and outrageous urges.

 Judith Viorst
(1931-) Poet, Journalist, Author

I remember adolescence, the years of having the impulse control of a mouse trap, of being as private as a safe deposit box.

 Anna Quindlen
(1953-) Novelist, Social Critic, Columnist

The average teenager still has all the faults his parents outgrew.

 Author Unknown

116

RELATING TO TEENS

Insightful Observations on
BECOMING A TEEN

HAVING BABIES

CHILDHOOD

TEENAGERS

PARENTING

HOME LIFE

RELATIVES

You know that children are growing up when they start asking questions that have answers.

 John J. Plomp
20th Century Writer,
Humorist

In many respects, the preteen years mimic adolescence, but without one essential ingredient: hormones.

 Laurence Balter
20th Century Psychologist,
Author; *Who's in Control?*

The trick, which requires the combined skills of a tightrope walker and a cordon bleu chef frying a plain egg, is to take your [preteen] daughter seriously without taking everything she says and does every minute seriously.

 Stella Chess
(1914-) Psychiatrist,
Professor of Child
Psychiatry, Author

We become adolescents when the words that adults exchange with one another become intelligible to us.

 Natalia Ginzburg
(1916-1991) Writer; *The Little Virtues*

Mother Nature is wonderful. She gives us twelve years to develop a love for our children before turning them into teenagers.

 Eugene P. Bertin
(1921-) Author, Scientist

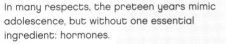 = IDEALIST   = REALIST   = CYNIC

117

RELATING TO TEENS

Insightful Observations on
TEEN REBELLION

Get out of my life, but first could you take me and Cheryl to the mall?

 Anthony E. Wolf
20th Century Author; *A Parent's Guide to the New Teenager*

If you want a baby, have a new one. Don't baby the old one.

 Jessamyn West
(1902-1984) Poet, Author

Young folks don't want you to understand 'em. You've got no more right to understand them than you have to play their games or wear their clothes.

 Edna Ferber
(1887-1968) Pulitzer Prize-winning Author

In high school, I was voted the girl most likely to become a nun. That may not be impressive to you, but it was quite an accomplishment at the Hebrew Academy.

 Rita Rudner
(1956-) Comedian

Much worse then rebellious teenagers are those who don't rebel and refuse to leave home.

 Bruce Lansky
Present Day Poet, Writer

My mother was afraid of me. I was so free-spirited, I was hard to control. She thought something horrible would happen to me. "You keep doing that and you'll end up a whore!"

 Kirstie Alley
(1951-) Actress

The young are generally full of revolt, and are often pretty revolting about it.

 Mignon McLaughlin
(1915-) Author; Journalist

RELATING TO TEENS

Insightful Observations on
TEENS ROLE IN FAMILY

HAVING BABIES

CHILDHOOD

TEENAGERS

PARENTING

HOME LIFE

RELATIVES

Adolescence is perhaps nature's way of preparing parents to welcome the empty nest.

 Karen Savage and Patricia Adams
Present Day Authors

No man knows his true character until he has run out of gas, purchased something on an installment plan and raised an adolescent.

 Marcelene Cox
20th Century Writer, Columnist

My friends complain that their teenagers sleep all day. Not me. Can you imagine if they were awake all day? Teenagers, like espresso, are meant to be taken in small doses.

 Buzz Nutley
Present Day Comedian

My little boys are growing up...
The baby's five-foot three!
It's great, but must they take such pride
In looking down on me?

 Susan D. Anderson
Present Day Psychologist, Educator

Little children, headache; big children, heartache.

 Italian Proverb

RELATING TO TEENS

Insightful Observations on
TEEN PROBLEMS

There is nothing wrong with today's teenager that twenty years won't cure.

 Author Unknown

It is hard to convince a high-school student that he will encounter a lot of problems more difficult than those of algebra and geometry.

 Edgar W. Howe
(1853-1937) American
Novelist

Like it's politicians and its wars, society has the teenagers it deserves.

 J.B. Priestley
(1894-1984) British
Journalist, Playwright,
Novelist, Essayist

Teenagers, are you tired of being harassed by your stupid parents? Act now. Move out, get a job, and pay your own bills—while you still know everything.

 John Hinde
Present Day Author

With any child entering adolescence, one hunts for signs of health, is desperate for the smallest indication that the child's problems will never be important enough for a television movie.

 Nora Ephron
(1941-) Writer, Director,
Producer

What is youth except a man or woman before it is ready or fit to be seen?

 Evelyn Waugh
(1903-1966) British Novelist

120

RELATING TO TEENS

Insightful Observations on
TEEN GIRL PROBLEMS

My eleven-year-old daughter mopes around the house waiting for her breasts to grow.

Bill Cosby
(1937-) Comedian, Actor, Producer

Any astronomer can predict with absolute accuracy just where every star in the universe will be at 11.30 tonight. He can make no such prediction about his teenage daughter.

James T. Adams
Present Day Humorist

There is a parallel between the twos and the tens. Tens are trying to test their abilities again, sizing up and experimenting to discover how to fit in. They don't mean everything they do and say. They are just testing…. Take a good deal of your daughter's behavior with a grain of salt. Try to handle the really outrageous as matter-of-factly as you would a mistake in grammar or spelling.

Stella Chess
(1914-) Author, Psychiatrist, Professor of Child Psychiatry

Having a teenage daughter is like being stuck in a hurricane. All you can do is board up your windows and look out in four years to see what the damage is.

Buzz Nutley
Present Day Comedian

Many a man wishes he were strong enough to tear a telephone book in half—especially if he has a teenage daughter.

Guy Lombardo
(1902-1977) Bandleader

Did you hear about the new teenage Barbie? You wind it up and it resents you.

Jay Trachman
Present Day Comedian, Author

INSIGHTFUL OBSERVATIONS TO SHARE

121

HAVING BABIES

CHILDHOOD

TEENAGERS

PARENTING

HOME LIFE

RELATIVES

RELATING TO TEENS

Insightful Observations on
TEEN BOY PROBLEMS

Teen-age boys who whistle at girls are just going through a stage which will probably last fifty years.

 Author Unknown

Young men are apt to think themselves wise enough, as drunken men are apt to think themselves sober enough.

 Lord Chesterfield
(1694-1773) British Writer, Statesman

Young men are fitter to invent than to judge, fitter for execution than for counsel, fitter for new projects than for settled business.

 Francis Bacon
(1561-1626) Renaissance Scholar, English Statesman, Essayist

I remember the first time I picked up my girlfriend at her parents' place. Her father said to me, "Make sure you have my daughter home by midnight." I said, "Don't worry, if it looks like I'm not getting anywhere, I'll have her home by ten."

 Stevie Ray Fromstein
Present Day Writer, Producer, Comedian

Today, only a fool would offer herself as the singular role model for the Good Mother. Most of us know not to tempt the fates. The moment I felt sure I had everything under control would invariably be the moment right before the principal called to report that one of my sons had just driven somebody's motorcycle through the high school gymnasium.

 Mary Kay Blakeley
Present Day Journalist, Author; *American Mom*

A boy becomes an adult three years before his parents think he does…and about two years after he thinks he does.

 Lewis Hershey
(1893-1977) U.S. Army General, Director of Selective Service

122

RELATING TO TEENS

Insightful Observations on
TEEN ANGST

HAVING BABIES

CHILDHOOD

TEENAGERS

PARENTING

HOME LIFE

RELATIVES

You don't have to suffer to be a poet. Adolescence is enough suffering for anyone.

John Ciardi
(1916- 1986) American Poet

Adolescence is a kind of emotional seasickness. Both are funny, but only in retrospect.

Arthur Koestler
(1905-1983) Novelist, Political Activist, Social Philosopher

Cult Leader: Are you a confused adolescent desperately seeking acceptance from an undifferentiated ego mass that demands conformity?

Family Guy
Animated TV Show (1999-2002)

At fourteen you don't need sickness or death for tragedy.

Jessamyn West
(1902-1984) Poet, Author

Adolescence is an awkward age in life for a youngster. They're too old for an allowance and too young for a credit card.

Author Unknown

 = IDEALIST  = REALIST = CYNIC

123

RELATING TO TEENS

Insightful Observations on
RELATING TO TEENS

Understanding does not necessarily mean agreement.

 Author Unknown

I love my kids, but I wouldn't want them as friends.

 Janet Sorenson
20th Century Author

I suppose you think that persons who are as old as your father and myself are always thinking about very grave things, but I know that we are meditating on the same old themes that we did when we were ten years old, only we go more gravely about them.

 Henry Thoreau
(1817-1862) Author, Poet; **to Ellen Emerson, Ralph Waldo Emerson's Daughter**

I firmly believe kids don't want your understanding. They want your trust, your compassion, your blinding love and your car keys, but you try to understand them and you're in big trouble.

 Erma Bombeck
(1927-1996) Humorist, Author

Adolescents are not monsters. They are just people trying to learn how to make it among the adults in the world, who are probably not so sure themselves.

 Virginia Satir
(1916-1988) Family Therapist, Author

Youth is something very new: twenty years ago no one mentioned it.

 Coco Chanel
(1883-1971) French Clothing Designer

It's difficult to decide whether growing pains are something teenagers have—or are.

 Author Unknown

124

RELATING TO TEENS

Insightful Observations on MANAGING TEENS

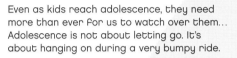

Even as kids reach adolescence, they need more than ever for us to watch over them... Adolescence is not about letting go. It's about hanging on during a very bumpy ride.

Ron Taffel
Present Day Psychologist, Author; *Why Parents Disagree*

Chaperons don't enforce morality; they force immorality to be discreet.

Judith Martin
(1938-) Etiquette Authority; pen name "Miss Manners"

God knows that a mother needs fortitude and courage and tolerance and flexibility and patience and firmness and nearly every other brave aspect of the human soul. But because I happen to be a parent of almost fiercely maternal nature, I praise casualness. It seems to me the rarest of virtues. It is useful enough when children are small. It is important to the point of necessity when they are adolescents.

Phyllis McGinley
(1905-1978) Author, Poet

If you want to recapture your youth, just cut off his allowance.

Al Bernstein
20th Century Psychologist, Columnist, Author

Between the ages of twelve and seventeen a parent can age thirty years.

Sam Levenson
(1911-1980) Humorist, Author

The best way to keep children home is to make the home atmosphere pleasant—and let the air out of the tires.

Dorothy Parker
(1893-1967) Author, Columnist, Poet

There is nothing wrong with teenagers that reasoning with them won't aggravate.

Robert Orben
(1927-) Author, Humorist

WELLNESS THROUGH LAUGHTER

HAVING BABIES

CHILDHOOD

TEENAGERS

PARENTING

HOME LIFE

RELATIVES

RELATING TO TEENS

Insightful Observations on NEGOTIATING WITH TEENS

I know that you believe you understand what you think I said, but I'm not sure you realize that what you heard is not what I meant.

Robert McCloskey
(1914-2003) Children's Author, Cartoonist

SHARON: Who did it?
KELLY: I'm not telling you.
SHARON: Why not?
KELLY: Because I know you're going to go down there and sue them.

Sharon Osborne
(1952-) to daughter Kelly Osborne (1984-) **about her Tattoo** in *The Osborne's* Reality TV Show

Too-broad questions, such as "What's on your mind?" are apt to be answered "nothing" nearly one hundred percent of the time. Be careful of slipping into "psycho-speak," however. Kids pick up instantly your attempt at being pseudo-shrink. Most resent it and are apt to tune out anything that sounds like you're reading a script from the latest child-psychology text.

Marge Kennedy
Present Day Author

Teenagers are people who act like babies if they're not treated like adults.

Mad Magazine

Teenagers are always ready to give adults the benefit of their inexperience

Author Unknown

Why should I be reasonable? I'm your mother.

Lynne Alpern & Esther Blumenfeld
Present Day Authors, Humorists; *Oh Lord, I Sound Just Like Mama*

SOCIAL LIFE

Insightful Observations on
TEEN SOCIAL LIFE

HAVING BABIES

CHILDHOOD

TEENAGERS

PARENTING

HOME LIFE

RELATIVES

As a teenager you are in the last stage of life when you will be happy to hear the phone is for you.

Fran Lebowitz
(1950-) Writer, Humorist

It's amazing. One day you look at your phone bill and realize they're teenagers.

Milton Berle
(1908-2002) Comedian, Actor, TV Personality

There used to be a saying that once your kid got old enough to help around the house, he was no longer around the house to help.

Theresa Bloomingdale
(1930-) Author

I am absolutely sure there is no life on Mars. It's not listed on my daughter's phone bills.

Larry Matthews
(1955-) Journalist

You know your children are growing up when they stop asking you where they came from and refuse to tell you where they're going.

P.J. O'Rourke
(1947-) Humorist, Journalist, Political Commentator

No need to worry about your teenagers when they're not at home. A national survey revealed that they all go to the same place—"out"—and they all do the same thing—"nothing."

Bruce Lansky
Present Day Poet, Writer

INSIGHTFUL OBSERVATIONS TO SHARE

HAVING BABIES

CHILDHOOD

TEENAGERS

PARENTING

HOME LIFE

RELATIVES

SOCIAL LIFE

Insightful Observations on
TEEN BOREDOM

Teenagers complain that there is nothing to do and then stay out all night getting it done.

 Author Unknown

REESE: I know I haven't been everywhere, but I'm pretty sure this is the most boring place on Earth.

 Justin Berfield
in *Malcolm in the Middle* TV Sitcom

So much of growing up is an unbearable waiting. A constant longing for another time. Another season.

 Sonia Sanchez
(1934-) Poet

And moreover my mother told me as a boy (repeatedly), "Ever to confess you're bored means you have no inner resources." I conclude now I have no inner resources, because I am very bored.

 John Berryman
(1914-1972) Poet

Mope-Hope-Grope

 Maxine Davis
20th Century Journalist, Writer; *The Lost Generation*

SOCIAL LIFE

Insightful Observations on
TEEN INDIVIDUALITY

HAVING BABIES

CHILDHOOD

TEENAGERS

PARENTING

HOME LIFE

RELATIVES

A youth is to be regarded with respect.

 Confucius
(551-479 B.C.) Chinese
Philosopher

I was always an observer. I would observe rather than partake, and I don't think that is too hip a thing to do when you're fifteen.

 Ruby Wax
(1953-) Actress, Comedian,
Writer

My daughter is a vegan and a Buddhist, and she won't wear a leather item anywhere on her body. There are things we do all over the place that, somehow, give the message to our children that you can make a difference and make a conscious choice.

 Jamie Lee Curtis
(1958-) Actress

GOTHIC is a 15-year old boy wearing a black skirt sitting on the floor in the corner of his room picking his pierced nose with a painted fingernail realizing that he is the only person on the planet who is sensitive and brilliant enough to fully comprehend the lyric 'hey, now, hey, now, now, sing this corrosion to me.'

 Author Unknown

Teenagers are people who express a burning desire to be different by dressing exactly alike.

 Author Unknown

A child develops individuality long before he develops taste.

 Erma Bombeck
(1927-1996) Humorist, Author

 = IDEALIST   = REALIST   = CYNIC

129

HAVING BABIES

CHILDHOOD

TEENAGERS

PARENTING

HOME LIFE

RELATIVES

SOCIAL LIFE

Insightful Observations on TEEN STYLE

I never expected to see the day when girls would get sunburned in the places they do now.

Will Rogers
(1878-1935) Humorist, Columnist, Actor

My dad used to tell me, "You know, you got to get a haircut," and I'd say, "What is the matter with the old man. Doesn't he know how cool I look?" But looking back at the prom pictures, I feel bad for every girl.

Adam Sandler
(1966-) Actor, Comedian, Producer

At the time we thought we looked fabulous, but now I look at those pictures and I want to kill myself.

Katie Couric
(1957-) Television Journalist

A teen-aged boy with spiked hair, nose ring and baggy clothes was overheard telling a friend, "I don't really like to dress like this, but it keeps my parents from dragging me everywhere with them."

Author Unknown

Eighteen-year-old kid, head shaved, both ears pierced, both nostrils pierced, both eyebrows pierced, tattoos coming out of the arms. He's got baggy pants that start at the knees, and twenty-seven inches of underwear. What's that about? That's one of the basic rules we know about—the underwear goes inside the pants! That's why it's called UNDER wear.

Denis Leary
(1957-) Comedian, Actor, Producer, Writer

You don't think times have changed? The Swiss Army knife has an ear-piercing tool on it.

George Carlin
(1938-) Comedian, Actor, Writer

130

SOCIAL LIFE

Insightful Observations on
TEEN ROLE MODELS

HAVING BABIES

CHILDHOOD

TEENAGERS

PARENTING

HOME LIFE

RELATIVES

Don't do drugs, don't have unprotected sex, don't be violent. Leave all that to me.

 Eminem
(1972-) Singer, Actor

Don't try to be like Jackie. There is only one Jackie...Study computers instead.

 Jackie Chan
(1954-) Chinese Actor

Young people need models, not critics.

 John Wooden
(1910-) UCLA Basketball Coach

It is the responsibility of every adult—especially parents, educators and religious leaders – to make sure that children hear what we have learned from the lessons of life and to hear over and over that we love them and they are not alone.

 Marian Wright Edelman
(1939-) Child Advocate, Author

I don't believe professional athletes should be role models. I believe parents should be role models... It's not like it was when I was growing up. My mom and my grandmother told me how it was going to be. If I didn't like it, they said, "Don't let the door hit you in the ass on your way out." Parents have to take better control.

 Charles Barkley
(1963-) Professional Basketball Player

Whatever I do, it's my business. It's not my job to parent America.

 Christina Aguilera
(1980-) Pop Singer, Songwriter

SOCIAL LIFE

Insightful Observations on
TEEN DRIVING

I remember when I was a teenager taking the car for a night out, sometimes my dad would take me aside and say, "Son here's an extra $271. Treat yourself to a car pool violation."

Bill Dwyer
Present Day Comedian, Actor

When buying a used car, punch the buttons on the radio. If all the stations are rock and roll, there's a good chance the transmission is shot.

Larry Lujack
(1940-) Radio Disc Jockey

The one thing that unites all human beings, regardless of age, gender, religion, economic status or economic background is that, deep down inside, we all believe that we are above average drivers.

Dave Barry
(1947-) Author, Humorist

In Toronto, a teenager was taking her driving test and crashed into six cars while trying to parallel park. She won't be able to drive in Canada, but on the bright side, she was issued a New York taxi license.

Conan O'Brien
(1963-) Humorist, Talk Show Host

In most states you can get a driver's license when you're sixteen years old, which made a lot of sense to me when I was sixteen years old but now seems insane.

Phyllis Diller
(1917-) Comedian, Actress, Author

Never lend your car to anyone to whom you have given birth.

Erma Bombeck
(1927-1996) Humorist, Author

SOCIAL LIFE

Insightful Observations on TEEN FRIENDS

HAVING BABIES

CHILDHOOD

TEENAGERS

PARENTING

HOME LIFE

RELATIVES

Friends aren't any more important than breath or blood to a high school senior.

 Betty Ford
(1918-) Wife of 38th U.S. President Gerald Ford

The young always have the same problem—how to rebel and conform at the same time. They have now solved this by defying their parents and copying one another.

 Quentin Crisp
(1908-1999) Actor, Writer, Model

Bringing up teenagers is like sweeping back ocean waves with a frazzled broom—the inundation of outside influences never stops.

 May Ellen Snodgrass
20th Century Writer

Debbie wasn't home and it was getting awfully late. Not knowing any of her girlfriend's phone numbers, her mother fired up Debbie's computer and saw a list of e-mail addresses. She sent a note to each name asking if they knew where her daughter was. Within twenty minutes, she got back 16 replies all saying that she wasn't to worry, that Debbie was spending the night at their house and had neglected to telephone.

 Author Unknown

There's a new book, Parents Don't Matter, which says that growing up, your peer group affects you more than your parents. I'm not sure I believe that. It's much easier to blame your parents. I still have their phone number.

 Norman K.
Present Day Comedian

INSIGHTFUL OBSERVATIONS TO SHARE

HAVING BABIES

CHILDHOOD

TEENAGERS

PARENTING

HOME LIFE

RELATIVES

SOCIAL LIFE

Insightful Observations on
TALKING ABOUT DRUGS

The best mind altering drug is truth.

Lily Tomlin
(1939-) Comedian, Actress

SON: Have you ever smoked opium?
FATHER: Certainly not! Gives you constipation. Dreadful binding effect. Ever see those pictures of the wretched poet Coleridge? Green around the gills. And a stranger to the lavatory. Avoid opium.

John Mortimer
(1923-) English Lawyer, Author, Dramatist

You cannot stop your kids from trying drugs, or even from abusing them, if that's what they decide to do. What you can do is practice honesty, equip your kids with accurate information about drugs, keep the doors of communication open by letting your kids know your love for them is unconditional, and remain nonjudgmental by creating a relationship where your kids feel safe to talk to you and get your input about their choices. When you abstain from judgments, your kids know that if they get into an abusive situation with their own experimentation, you will be there with honesty, love and support that is empowering instead of enabling.

Jane Nelson
20th Century Educational Psychologist, Writer

It's not called cocaine anymore. It's now referred to as "Crack Classic."

Billiam Coronel
Present Day Comedian, Writer, Producer

My father told me marijuana would cause me brain damage—because if he caught me doing it he was going to break my head.

Tom Dreesen
(1942-) Actor, Comedian

I'd stay away from Ecstasy. This is a drug so strong it makes white people think they can dance.

Lenny Henry
(1958-) British Entertainer

134

TEEN DATING

Insightful Observations on
COMING OF AGE

The best substitute for experience is being sixteen.

Raymond Duncan
20th Century Author

The age of puberty is a crisis—it is a passage from the unconscious to the conscious; from the sleep of the passion to their rage; from careless receiving to cunning providing.

Ralph Waldo Emerson
(1803-1882) Author, Poet, Philosopher

There are children born to be children, and others who must mark time till they can take their natural place as adults.

Mignon McLaughlin
(1915-) Author, Journalist

During adolescence, imagination is boundless.

Louise Kaplan
20th Century Author, Psychologist

"You kids think you invented sex," my mother was fond of saying. But hadn't we? With no instruction manual or federally-enforced training period, didn't we all come away feeling we'd discovered something unspeakably modern?

David Sedaris
(1957-) Writer, Radio Commentator

Adolescence is to life what baking powder is to cake.

Marcelene Cox
20th Century Writer, Columnist

Quite a few women told me, one way or another, that they thought it was sex, not youth, that's wasted on the young…

Jean Harris
(1931-) Politician, Physician

 = IDEALIST   = REALIST   = CYNIC

135

HAVING BABIES

CHILDHOOD

TEENAGERS

PARENTING

HOME LIFE

RELATIVES

TEEN DATING

Insightful Observations on
GIRLS COMING OF AGE

Because her need to love and be loved is smoldering and constant as a vestal fire, the young female is more randy than the male, whose lust rises and falls according to what is on offer.

Irma Kurtz
(1935-) Author

An actress reading a part for the first time tries many ways to say the same line before she settles into the one she believes suits the character and situation best. There's an aspect of the rehearsing actress that's like a girl on the verge of her teens.

Stella Chess
(1914-) Psychiatrist, Professor of Child Psychiatry, Author

Girlhood…is the intellectual phase of a woman's life, that time when, unencumbered by societal expectations or hormonal rages, one may pursue any curiosity from the mysteries of a yo-yo to the meaning of infinity. These two particular pursuits were where I left off in the fifth grade when I discovered a hair growing in the wrong place and all hell broke loose.

Alice Kahn
(1940-) Author, Essayist

From the moment I was six I felt sexy. And let me tell you it was hell, sheer hell, waiting to do something about it.

Bette Davis
(1908-1989) Actress

I've just been to a debutant ball where all the girls were wearing low-cut gowns. It's clear why they're called coming out parties.

Martin Fenton
20th Century Humorist

136

TEEN DATING

Insightful Observations on
BOYS COMING OF AGE

HAVING BABIES

CHILDHOOD

TEENAGERS

PARENTING

HOME LIFE

RELATIVES

Perhaps at fourteen every boy should be in love with some ideal woman to put on a pedestal and worship. As he grows up, of course, he will put her on a pedestal the better to view her legs.

Barry Norman
(1933-) British Cinema Critic

I'm obsessed with girls. When you're my age your hormones are just kicking in and there's not much besides sex on your mind.

Leonardo DiCaprio
(1974-) Actor; **as a teenager**

The big mistake men make is that when they turn thirteen or fourteen and all of a sudden they've reached puberty, they believe that they like women. Actually, you're just horny. It doesn't mean you like women any more at twenty-one than you did at ten.

Jules Feiffer
(1929-) Cartoonist, Playwright

Boys will be boys—and even that wouldn't matter if we could only prevent girls from being girls.

Anthony Hope
(1863-1933) British Novelist

WELLNESS THROUGH LAUGHTER

TEEN DATING

Insightful Observations on
TEEN CHILDREN DATING

Watching your daughter being collected by her date feels like handing over a million dollar Stradivarius to a gorilla.

 Jim Bishop
Present Day Comedian, Writer

Imagination is something that sits up with Dad and Mom the first time their teenager stays out late.

 Lane Olinghouse
20th Century Writer

Puberty is the stage children reach that gets parents to start worrying about pregnancy all over again.

 Joyce Armor
Present Day Writer

I have adapted the philosophy of Genghis Khan, "Give a man fish, and he eats for a day; teach a man to fish and he eats for a lifetime," for my slogan: "Show a teenage boy a gun, and he'll have your daughter home before 11:30 p.m."

 Sinbad
(1956-) Comedian, Actor, Writer

138

TEEN DATING

Insightful Observations on
DATING ADVICE FOR GIRLS

HAVING BABIES

CHILDHOOD

TEENAGERS

PARENTING

HOME LIFE

RELATIVES

Don't let a fool kiss you, or a kiss fool you.

Gladiola Montana and Texas Bix Bender
Presnt Day Authors

Distrust all those who love you extremely upon a very slight acquaintance and without any visible reason.

Lord Chesterfield
(1694-1773) British Writer, Statesman

My advice to girls: first, don't smoke—to excess; second, don't drink—to excess; third, don't marry—to excess.

Mark Twain
(1835-1910) Writer, Humorist

Never mistake motion for action.

Ernest Hemingway
(1899-1961) Author

Boys don't make passes at female smart-asses.

Letty Cottin
Pogrebin (1939-) Journalist, Women's Movement Leader

Don't accept rides from strange men—and remember that all men are strange as hell.

Robin Morgan
(1941-) Editor; Ms Magazine

INSIGHTFUL OBSERVATIONS TO SHARE

HAVING BABIES

CHILDHOOD

TEENAGERS

PARENTING

HOME LIFE

RELATIVES

TEEN DATING

Insightful Observations on
DATING ADVICE FOR BOYS

Women are like banks, boy. Breaking and entering is a serious business.

Joe Orton
(1933-1967) British Dramatist

Never let the little head do the thinking for the big head.

Author Unknown

Never eat at a place called Mom's. Never play cards with a man named Doc. And never lie down with a woman who's got more troubles than you.

Nelson Algren
(1909-1981) Novelist

I have heard a well built woman compared in her motion to a ship under sail, yet I would advise no wise man to be her owner if her freight be nothing but what she carries between wind and water.

Francis Osborne
(1751-1799) Essayist; **advising his son not to marry a beautiful but dumb girl**

Never mistake endurance for hospitality.

Author Unknown

TEEN DATING

Insightful Observations on
FIRST LOVE

HAVING BABIES

CHILDHOOD

TEENAGERS

PARENTING

HOME LIFE

RELATIVES

First love is only a little foolishness and a lot of curiosity.

George Bernard Shaw
(1856-1950) Playwright, Novelist, Critic

Every young girl tries to smother her first love in possessiveness. Oh what tears and rejection await the girl who imbues her first delicate match with fantasies of permanence, expecting that he at this gelatinous stage will fit with her in a finished puzzle for all the days.

Gail Sheehy
(1937-) Writer, Journalist, Editor

My parents actually met in junior high school. I guess they figured: What the heck, once you've seen someone in junior high, you've pretty much seen them at their worst.

Norman K.
Present Day Comedian

Men always want to be a woman's first love. That is their clumsy vanity. We women have a more subtle instinct about things. What we like is to be a man's last romance.

Oscar Wilde
(1854-1900) Poet, Playwright, Novelist; *from A Woman of No Importance*

A man always remembers his first love with special tenderness, but after that he begins to bunch them.

H.L. Mencken
(1880-1956) Editor, Writer

At seventeen you tend to go for unhappy love affairs.

Francoise Sagan
(1935-) Novelist

 = IDEALIST  = REALIST = CYNIC

TEEN DATING

Insightful Observations on
LEARNING ABOUT SEX

From best sellers to comic books (or, from TV and the Internet), any child who hasn't acquired an extensive sex education by the age of 12 belongs in remedial reading.

Will Stanton
(1918-) Author

Through that dear little village,
Surrounded by trees,
Had neither a school nor a college,
Gentle Alice acquired from birds and the bees
Some exceedingly practical knowledge.

Noel Coward
(1899-1964) English Actor,
Dramatist,

And while we're at it, let's teach a follow-up class to sex education. Call if Reality 101 — hammering home to a sixteen-year-old teen that he or she is going to have to quit school, quit video games, quit hanging out, and work a fifty-hour week dumping frozen chicken tenders into hot oil just so you can keep little Scooter Junior in Similac. Trust me, that's a bigger deterrent to teenage sex than the backseat of a Yugo.

Dennis Miller
(1953-) Actor, Comedian

If sex is such a natural phenomenon, how come there are so many books on how to?

Bette Midler
(1944-) Actress, Singer,
Comedian

Nobody should die of ignorance.

Elizabeth Taylor
(1932-) Actress

I don't worry too much about sex education in the schools. If the kids learn it like they do everything else, they won't know how.

Milton Berle
(1908-2002) Comedian,
Actor, TV Personality

142

TEEN DATING

Insightful Observations on SAFE SEX

Contraceptives should be used on every conceivable occasion.

Spike Milligan
(1918-) British Comic Actor, Author

I want to tell you a terrific story about oral contraception. I asked this girl to sleep with me and she said no.

Woody Allen
(1935-) Director, Actor, Writer

Put 200 condoms in a box someplace in the house where everybody isn't all the time, so that your kids can take them.

Sharon Stone
(1958-) Actress, Model, Producer

Safe sex is very important. That's why I'm never doing it on a plywood scaffolding again.

Jenny Jones
(1946-) TV Talk Show Host

Mother, you who conceived without sinning, teach me how to sin without conceiving.

Author Unknown

There's a new birth-control pill for women. You put it between your knees and keep it there.

Bill Barner
Present Day Comedian

For a single woman, the most effective method of oral contraception is to just yell out, Yes, yes, I want to have your baby!!!

Marsha Doble
Present Day Comedian

HAVING BABIES

CHILDHOOD

TEENAGERS

PARENTING

HOME LIFE

RELATIVES

TEEN DATING

Insightful Observations on
COMMUNICATING ABOUT SEX

It's not about sex education anymore, it's about sex planning.

 Oscar Herman
(1909-1980) Humorist, Shoe Salesman

My favorite book when I was eight was *Everything You Always Wanted To Know About Sex—But Where Afraid To Ask*. I was not afraid to ask.

 Drew Barrymore
(1975-) Actress, Producer

Neither Papa nor Mama nor the schools taught me about sex, at least not officially. I wanted to know, but no one sat down to give me a sex organ recital. Mama certainly couldn't do it, in spite of the fact that she had given birth to ten children. When asked if she had ever heard of "sex appeal", she said, "I gave already."

 Sam Levenson
(1911-1980) Humorist, Author

Baby Boomer father talking to his son: You'd better ask your grandparents about that, son—my generation is very uncomfortable talking about abstinence.

 Robert Mankoff
Present Day Cartoonist in *New Yorker*

My daughters and I have a deal where they are not allowed to have sex until after I'm dead.

 Billy Crystal
(1947-) Actor, Comedian

When mom found my diaphragm I told her it was a bathing cap for my cat.

 Liz Winston
Present Day Comedian, Author

Telling a teenager the facts of life is like giving a fish a bath.

 Arnold H. Glasow
20th Century Philosopher

TEEN DATING

Insightful Observations on
GAY CHILDREN

HAVING BABIES

CHILDHOOD

TEENAGERS

PARENTING

HOME LIFE

RELATIVES

Using the word "gay" as a euphemism for homosexual is fine, I guess. But I've always thought a word like "fabulous" might even have been better. Sure would be a lot easier to tell your parents, "Mom, Dad – I'm FABULOUS! And my friends are fabulous too!

Michael Greer
(1943-2002) Comedian,
Actor, Composer

My high school had a Head Start program for homosexuals – it was called Drama Club.

Bob Smith
Present Day Comedian,
Author

...The whole point of what I'm doing is acceptance of everyone's differences. It's just that I don't want them representing the entire gay community, and I'm sure they don't want me representing them. We're individuals.

Ellen Degeneres
(1958-) Actor, Comedian,
Talk Show Host; **on
revealing she is gay,**

My parents were in denial about my being gay. I wasn't afraid of the dark, I was afraid of unflattering light.

Bob Smith
Present Day Comedian,
Author

The most difficult thing for me in coming out was how I was going to record my parents reaction, I was going to film school and it was my class project.

Heather Stobo
(1969-) Writer,
Photographer

There's been a lot of speculation about what causes homosexuality. So far, no one seems to know. Although in our family, I was the only one who would drink strawberry-flavored Nestle's Quik.

Bob Smith
Present Day Comedian,
Author

The next time someone asks you, "Hey, howdja get to be a homosexual anyway?" tell them, "Homosexuals are chosen first on talent, then interview. The swimsuit and evening gown competition pretty much gets rid of the rest of them."

Karen Williams
Present Day Comedian

INSIGHTFUL OBSERVATIONS TO SHARE

HAVING BABIES

CHILDHOOD

TEENAGERS

PARENTING

HOME LIFE

RELATIVES

KIDS LEAVING HOME

Insightful Observations on
GROWING-UP

There is always a moment in childhood when the door opens and lets the future in.

 Deepak Chopra
(1947-) Physician, Author;
Founder of Transcendental
Meditation Movement

Real Mothers know that a child's growth is not measured by height or years or grade... It is marked by the progression of Mama to Mommy to Mother.

 Author unknown

A child becomes an adult when he realizes that he has a right not only to be right but also to be wrong.

 Thomas Szasz
(1920-) Psychiatrist

What parent ever thought a child had arrived at maturity?

Mary Clavers
(1801-1864) Writer

It kills you to see them grow up. But I guess it would kill you quicker if they didn't.

Barbara Kingsolver
(1955-) Novelist

The Jewish man with parents still alive is a fifteen year old boy and will remain a fifteen year old boy until they die.

 Philip Roth
(1933-) Author

We've had bad luck with our kids. They've all grown up.

 Christopher Morley
(1890-1957) Author;
Journalist

KIDS LEAVING HOME

Insightful Observations on LEAVING HOME

What is a home without children? Quiet.

 Henny Youngman
(1906-1998) Comedian, Violinist

You see much more of your children once they leave home.

 Lucille Ball
(1911-1989) Actress, Writer, Producer

There are two lasting bequests we can give our children. One is roots. The other is wings.

 Hodding Carter
(1907-1972) Journalist

God lends you your children until they're about eighteen years old. If you haven't made your point by then, it's too late.

 Betty Ford
(1918-) Wife of 38th U.S. President Gerald Ford

When mothers talk about the depression of the empty nest, they're not mourning the passing of all those wet towels on the floor, or the music that numbs their teeth, or even the bottle of cap less shampoo dribbling down the shower drain. They're upset because they've gone from supervisor of a child's life to a spectator. It's like being the vice president of the United States.

Erma Bombeck
(1927-1996) Humorist, Author

I gave my son a hint. On his room door I put a sign: CHECKOUT TIME IS 18.

 Milton Berle
(1908-2002) Comedian, Actor, TV Personality

Life does not begin at the moment of conception or the moment of birth. It begins when the kids leave home and the dog dies.

 Author Unknown

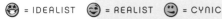 = IDEALIST   = REALIST   = CYNIC

147

KIDS LEAVING HOME

Insightful Observations on
CHOOSING A COLLEGE

Helping your eldest to pick a college is one of the greatest educational experiences of life—for the parents. Next to trying to pick his bride, it's the best way to learn that your authority, if not entirely gone, is slipping fast.

Sally F. Reston (1914-2003) and James Reston (1909- 1995) Journalists

College football is a sport that bears the same relation to education that bullfighting does to agriculture.

Elbert Hubbard (1856-1915) Author, Publisher

Fathers send their sons to college either because they went to college or they didn't.

L.L. Hendren 20th Century Author

I have a daughter who goes to S.M.U. She could've gone to U.C.L.A. here in California, but it's got one more letter she'd have to remember.

Shecky Greene (1926-) Actor, Comedian

KIDS LEAVING HOME

Insightful Observations on
ATTENDING COLLEGE

College is the best time of your life. When else are your parents going to spend several thousand dollars a year just for you to go to a strange town and get drunk every night?

David Wood
20th Century Humorist, Author

If you have a college degree you can be absolutely sure of one thing...you have a college degree.

Author Unknown

College is a place to keep warm between high school and an early marriage.

George Gobel
(1919-1991) Actor, Humorist

Last words when sending our boy to college: "If there is anything you want, call us and we will show you how to live without it"

Author Unknown

When I went to college, my parents threw a going-away party for me, according to the letter.

Emo Philips
Present Day Comedian

HAVING BABIES

CHILDHOOD

TEENAGERS

PARENTING

HOME LIFE

RELATIVES

HAVING BABIES

CHILDHOOD

TEENAGERS

PARENTING

HOME LIFE

RELATIVES

KIDS LEAVING HOME

Insightful Observations on
COMING BACK HOME

Human beings are the only creatures on earth that allow their children to come back home.

 Bill Cosby
(1937-) Comedian, Actor, Producer

People think living in your parent's basement until you're twenty-nine is lame. But what they don't realize is that while you're there, you save more on rent, food, and dates.

 Ray Romano
(1957-) Actor, Comedian

The way to cure homesickness is to go home.

 Edna Ferber
(1887-1968) Pulitzer Prize-winning Author

There isn't a child who hasn't gone out into the brave new world who eventually doesn't return to the old homestead carrying a bundle of dirty clothes.

 Art Buchwald
(1925-) Author, Columnist, Dramatist, Journalist

There is no way that moving in with your parents is a sign your life is on track.

 Jerry Seinfeld
(1954-) Comedian, Actor, Producer

Thomas Wolfe wrote, "You can't go home again." You can, but you'll get treated like an eight-year-old.

 Daryl Hogue
Present Day Comedian

Insightful Observations

HAVING BABIES

CHILDHOOD

TEENAGERS

PARENTING

HOME LIFE

RELATIVES

_____

_____

_____

_____

_____

_____

_____

_____

_____

_____

_____

_____

_____

_____

_____

_____

_____

INSIGHTFUL OBSERVATIONS TO SHARE

Step Four:

PARE

NTING

Parenthood
Fatherhood
Motherhood

HAVING BABIES

CHILDHOOD

TEENAGERS

PARENTING

HOME LIFE

RELATIVES

PARENTHOOD

Insightful Observations on
THE JOY OF PARENTHOOD

There is nothing more fulfilling in this world, I think, than having a child that is yours, and yet is mysteriously a stranger.

 Agatha Christie
(1891-1976) Author

To show a child what has once delighted you, to find the child's delight added to your own, so that there is now a double delight seen in the glow of trust and affection, this is happiness.

J.B. Priestley
(1894-1984) British
Journalist, Playwright,
Novelist, Essayist

I have found the happiness of parenthood greater than any other that I have experienced.

 Bertrand Russell
(1872-1970) Philosopher,
Mathematician

The joys of parents are secret, and so are their grief's and fears.

Francis Bacon
(1909-1992) Designer,
Painter

There are times when parenthood seems nothing but feeding the mouth that bites you.

Peter De Vries
(1910-1993) Editor, Writer

Children really brighten up a household— they never turn the lights off.

Ralph Bus
20th Century Humorist

Kids: they're not easy, but there has to be some penalty for sex.

Bill Maher
(1956-) Writer, TV Talk Show
Host

154

PARENTHOOD

Insightful Observations on
PARENTAL ROLES

HAVING BABIES

CHILDHOOD

TEENAGERS

PARENTING

HOME LIFE

RELATIVES

Nurses nurse, and teachers teach, and tailors mend, and preachers preach, and barbers trim, and chauffeurs haul, and parents get to do it all.

Babs Bell Hajdusiewicz
(1944-) Children's Author, Poet, Educator

The job of a parent is to eventually do himself out of a job.

Alice Freedman
20th Century Parent Educator

There are three main parenting jobs: getting your kid to go to sleep without bedtime problems, getting your kid to eat without being finicky, and getting your kid toilet trained. Nobody I know has scored three out of three.

Keisha
Present Day Clothing Designer

It's 10 p.m. Do you know where your children are?

U.S. Public Service Announcement

"Equal parenting" does not work—the maternal fine-tuning never turns off.

Phyllis Schlafly
(1924-) American Author, Political Activist

My mother protected me from the world and my father threatened me with it.

Quentin Crisp
(1908-1999) Actor, Writer, Model

Three stages in a parent's life: Nutrition, dentition, tuition.

Marcelene Cox,
20th Century Writer, Columnist

 = IDEALIST = REALIST = CYNIC

PARENTHOOD

Insightful Observations on
UNDERSTANDING PARENTS

Are anybody's parents typical?

😊 Madeleine L'Engle
(1918-) Author

Parents talking as kids play around them: "Like everyone else these days, we've made most of our friends through our kids."

😊 Lee Lorenz
Present Day Cartoonist in *The New Yorker*

When your mother asks, "Do you want a piece of advice?" it's a mere formality. It doesn't matter if you answer yes or no. You're going to get it anyway.

😊 Erma Bombeck
(1927-1996) Humorist, Author

You want to hear the childhood daredevil stories my mother tells company? "Once a glass broke on the kitchen floor, not one week later my daughter was in there without her shoes on." I broke a glass in 1954, they sold the house in 1985, my mother warned the new owners, "I think I got all the big pieces, but there could be slivers."

😊 Elayne Boosler
(1952-) Comedian, Actress

Adults are always asking children what they want to be when they grow up—they're looking for ideas.

😊 Paula Poundstone
(1959-) Comedian, Writer, Actress

Parents are the bones on which children sharpen their teeth.

😊 Peter Ustinov
(1921-) British Writer, Actor

PARENTHOOD

Insightful Observations on
PARENTAL NURTURING

HAVING BABIES

CHILDHOOD

TEENAGERS

PARENTING

HOME LIFE

RELATIVES

My father gave me the greatest gift anyone could give another person. He believed in me.

Jim Valvano
(1946-1993) College Basketball Coach; NC State

Envy the kangaroo. The pouch setup is extraordinary; the baby crawls out of the womb when it is about two inches long, gets into the pouch, and proceeds to mature. I'd have a baby if it would develop in my handbag.

Rita Rudner
(1956-) Comedian

Do everything right, all the time, and the child will prosper. It is as simple as that, except for fate, luck, heredity, chance and the astrological sign under which the child was born, his birth order, his first encounter with evil, the girl who jilts him in spite of his excellent qualities, the war that is being fought when he is a young man, the drugs he may try once or too many times, the friends he makes, how he scores on tests, how well he endures kidding about his shortcomings, how ambitious he becomes, how far he falls behind, circumstantial evidence, ironic perspective, danger when it's least expected, difficulty in triumphing over circumstance, people with hidden agendas, and animals with rabies.

Ann Beattie
(1947-) Writer

We love those we feed, not vise versa; in caring for others we nourish our own self esteem.

Jessamyn West
(1902-1984) Poet, Author

HAVING BABIES

CHILDHOOD

TEENAGERS

PARENTING

HOME LIFE

RELATIVES

PARENTHOOD

Insightful Observations on
PARENTAL LOVE

Nobody has ever measured, even poets, how much a heart can hold.

Zelda Fitzgerald
(1900-1948) Artist, Writer, Dancer

If you were arrested for being a loving parent, would there be enough evidence to convict you?

Author Unknown

The greatest weakness of most humans is their hesitancy to tell others how much they love them while they're alive.

O.A. Battista
(1901-1973) Canadian Author, Chemist

You don't know what love is until you become a parent. You don't know what love is until you fish a turd out of the bathtub for someone.

Margaret Smith
20th Century Comedian

How then do you love each of your multiple children, if not the best or even equally? The answer is, you love them uniquely.

Marianne E. Neifert
Pediatrician, Author, *Dr. Mom's Parenting Guide* (1991)

I love all my children, but some of them I don't like.

Lillian Carter
(1902-1983) Mother of Jimmy Carter; 29th U.S. President

My unhealthy affection for my second daughter has waned. Now I despise all my seven children equally.

Evelyn Waugh
(1903-1966) British Novelist

PARENTHOOD

Insightful Observations on
PARENTAL SACRIFICE

HAVING BABIES

CHILDHOOD

TEENAGERS

PARENTING

HOME LIFE

RELATIVES

The only reward for love is the experience of loving.

John LeCarré
(1931-) British Spy Novelist

Fatherhood was full-time work for Dad. When I was about ten, I took up the clarinet. Instead of buying me a metronome or sending me off to a soundproof room to squeak my way through the scales, he sat with me and beat time against the arm of his chair with his pipe.

William G. Tapply
(1940-) Editor, Author

The debt of gratitude we owe our mother and father goes forward, not backward. What we owe our parents is the bill presented to us by our children.

Nancy Friday
(1937-) Writer, Psychologist

Today's fathers and mothers—with only the American dream for guidance—extend and overextend themselves, physically, emotionally, and financially, during the best years of their lives to ensure that their children will grow up prepared to do better and go further than they did.

Stella Chess
Present Day Author,
Professor of Child Psychiatry

You give up, or postpone, many of the pleasures you once enjoyed, such as eating when you are hungry…going to sleep when you are tired.

Lydia Davis
Present Day Author

I was asking my friend who has children, "What if I have a baby and I dedicate my life to it and it grows up to hate me. And it blames everything wrong with its life on me." And she said, "What do you mean, 'If'?"

Rita Rudner
(1956-) Comedian

HAVING BABIES

CHILDHOOD

TEENAGERS

PARENTING

HOME LIFE

RELATIVES

PARENTHOOD

Insightful Observations on
PARENTAL PRIDE

A mother's children are portraits of herself. Author Unknown

Likely as not, the child you can do the least with will do the most to make you proud. Mignon McLaughlin
(1915-) Author, Journalist

All parents believe their children can do the impossible. They thought it the minute we were born, and no matter how hard we've tried to prove them wrong, they all think it about us now. And the really annoying thing is, they're probably right. Cathy Guisewite
(1950-) Cartoonist; Cathy

Viewers watch us in quick blips, when they're brushing their teeth, packing their kids off to school, running on the treadmill, those are the best ones: They watch us for 20 minutes. Only my Mom and Dad watch from beginning to end. Katie Couric
(1957-) Television Journalist

Sometimes when I look at all my children, I say to myself, "Lillian, you should have stayed a virgin." Lillian Carter
(1902-1983) Mother of Jimmy Carter, 39th U.S. President

I don't want to say anything about my kids, but I go to PTA meetings under an assumed name! Robert Orben
(1927-) Author, Humorist

The fundamental defect of fathers is that they want their children to be a credit to them. Bertrand Russell
(1872-1970) Philosopher, Mathematician

PARENTHOOD

Insightful Observations on PARENTAL BRAGGING

John Elway is a great football player. He used to be my son. Now I'm his father.

 Jack Elway
(1932-2001) Football Coach

Parents of young children should realize that few people, and maybe no one, will find their children as enchanting as they do.

Barbara Walters
(1931-) News Correspondent, Producer

I couldn't throw a ball. There's a problem you see in an Irish Catholic family. The boy that can't throw the ball is going to be the priest.

John McGivern
Present Day Comedian, Writer, Actor

My dad didn't like people as much as he liked his car. He even introduced it to people. "It's my Bonneville," he said. "My family's over there." Then he went on, "It's an American-made car. You can drive it head-on into a train and live."

Louie Anderson
(1953-) Comedian, Actor, Writer

Once you have children, it forever changes the way you bore other people.

Bruce Eric Kaplan
Present Day Cartoonist in *The New Yorker*

Dad named his first ulcer after me.

Author Unknown

My kid had sex with your honor student.

Bumper sticker

😄 = IDEALIST   😊 = REALIST   🙂 = CYNIC

161

HAVING BABIES

CHILDHOOD

TEENAGERS

PARENTING

HOME LIFE

RELATIVES

PARENTHOOD

Insightful Observations on
PARENTAL WORRY

One of the oldest human needs is having someone to wonder where you are when you don't come home at night.

Margaret Mead
(1901-1978) Anthropologist

It's like the smarter you are, the more things can scare you.

Katherine Paterson
(1932-) Children's Author

My father died at 102. Whenever I would ask him what kept him going, he'd answer, "I never worry."

Jerry Stiller
(1927-) Comedian, Actor

Worry is interest paid on trouble before it comes due.

William R. Inge
(1860-1954) Dean of St. Paul's, London

Children will do what they need to do when they are ready—they cannot do things until then—enjoy them, don't worry. Let them tell you when they are ready for more. Enjoy your children's childhood—it doesn't last long.

Author Unknown

If you don't have children, the longing for them will kill you, and if you do, the worrying over them will kill you.

Buchi Emecheta
(1944-) African Writer

Diagnosis According to a Mother Mind:
Child has a runny nose...brain tumor
Child has a headache...brain tumor
Child has a funny spot on arm...arm tumor

Amy Krouse
Rosenthal Present Day Writer, Columnist, Mother

162

PARENTHOOD

Insightful Observations on
PARENTAL DISCRETION

Parents should conduct their arguments in quiet, respectful tones, but in a foreign language. You'd be surprised what an inducement that is to the education of children.

 Judith Martin
(1938-) Etiquette Authority; pen name "Miss Manners"

If you don't want your children to hear what you are saying, pretend you're talking to them.

Author Unknown

My first-grade teacher said, "Okay, Mark, tell us everything you know about the letter H." I said, "That's Jesus's middle name."

Mark Lundholm
Present Day Comedian

My list of things I never pictured myself saying when I pictured myself as a parent has grown over the years.

Polly Berrien Berends
Present Day Author; *Whole Child/Whole Parent*

Being a parent is such serious business that we dare not take it too seriously. Children are inherently funny. So are parents. We all are at our funniest when we are desperately struggling to appear to be in control of a new situation.

Lawrence Kutner,
Ph.D 20th Century Psychologist, Author, Columnist, Professor

HAVING BABIES

CHILDHOOD

TEENAGERS

PARENTING

HOME LIFE

RELATIVES

PARENTHOOD

Insightful Observations on
PARENTAL EXPECTATIONS

My mother wanted me to be her wings, to fly as she never quite had the courage to do.

Erica Jong
(1942-) Writer, Poet

I want my children to have all the things I couldn't afford. Then I want to move in with them.

Phyllis Diller
(1917-) Comedian, Actress, Author

My father the banker would shudder to see, in the back of his bank a painter to be.

Paul Cezanne
(1839-1906) French Painter

A father is a man who expects his son to be as good a man as he meant to be.

Frank. A. Clark
20th Century Author

My parent's dream was for me to have everything they didn't. And thanks to ozone holes, fear of AIDS, and no health insurance, their dream has come true.

Brad Slaight
Present day Actor, Writer, Comedian

My mother was always unhappy with what I do. She would rather I do something nicer, like be a bricklayer.

Mick Jagger
(1943-) Lead Singer; The Rolling Stones

I phoned my dad to tell him I stopped smoking. He called me a quitter.

Steven Pearl
Present Day Comedian, Humorist

PARENTHOOD

Insightful Observations on
PARENTAL FAULTS

HAVING BABIES

CHILDHOOD

TEENAGERS

PARENTING

HOME LIFE

RELATIVES

The first time I lied to my baby, I told him that it was his face on the baby food jar.

Maxine Chernoff
(1952-) American Novelist

Parents don't make mistakes because they don't care, but because they care so deeply.

T. Berry Brazelton
(1918-) Pediatrician, Author

I didn't make the same mistakes my parents made when they raised me. I was too busy making new ones.

Bruce Lansky
Present Day Poet, Writer

Blaming mother is just a negative way of clinging to her still.

Nancy Friday
(1937-) Writer, Psychologist

Children find comfort in flaws, ignorance, insecurities similar to their own. I love my mother for letting me see hers.

Erma Bombeck
(1927-1996) Humorist, Author

Parents are sometimes a bit of a disappointment to their children. They don't fulfill the promise of their early years.

Anthony Powell
(1905-) British Novelist

They f_ _k you up, your Mum and Dad.
They may not mean to, but they do.
And give you all the faults they had.
And add some extra, just for you.

Philip Larkin
(1922-1985) British Poet

INSIGHTFUL OBSERVATIONS TO SHARE

165

HAVING BABIES

CHILDHOOD

TEENAGERS

PARENTING

HOME LIFE

RELATIVES

PARENTHOOD

Insightful Observations on
PARENTAL ADVICE

Mother Knows Best.

 Edna Ferber
(1887-1968) Journalist,
Author, Actor

Write down the advice of him who loves you, though you like it not at present.

 English Proverb

I have found the best way to give advice to your children is to find out what they want and then advise them to do it.

 Harry S. Truman
(1884-1972) 33rd U.S.
President

Have no respect whatsoever for authority; forget who said it and instead look at what he starts with, where he ends up, and ask yourself, "Is it reasonable?"

 Fatherly advice to
Richard Feyman
(1918-1988) Nobel Prize
Winning Physicist

No one wants advice—only corroboration.

 John Steinbeck
(1902-1968) Novelist

If at first you don't succeed, do it like your mother told you.

 Author Unknown

No matter what, Dad was always there with solid words of advice—"go ask your mother."

 Alan Ray
20th Century Humorist,
Educator

166

PARENTHOOD

Insightful Observations on
PARENTAL LEARNING

HAVING BABIES

CHILDHOOD

TEENAGERS

PARENTING

HOME LIFE

RELATIVES

Parents learn a lot from their children about coping with life.

 Muriel Spark
(1918-) Scottish-Born Writer

…Having two children. Without any question, it's made me a better actor and a better person.

 Rob Lowe
(1964-) Actor, Producer

We learn from experience. Man never wakes up his second baby just to see it smile.

 Grace Williams
(1906-1977) Welsh Composer

Things my children taught me: A 4 year-old's voice is louder than 200 adults in a crowded restaurant. A magnifying glass can start a fire even on an overcast day. A king size waterbed holds enough water to fill a 2000 sq foot house 4 inches deep. Legos will pass through the digestive tract of a four year old. Always look in the oven before you turn it on. If you spray hair spray on dust bunnies and run over them with roller blades, they can ignite.

Author Unkown

You can learn many things from children. How much patience you have, for instance.

 Franklin P. Jones
(1853-1935) Entertainer

Grown-ups never understand anything for themselves, and it is tiresome for children to be always and forever explaining things to them.

 Antoine de Saint-Exupery
(1900-1944) French Author, Poet

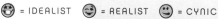 = IDEALIST   = REALIST = CYNIC

PARENTHOOD

Insightful Observations on
BEING FAIR

Parents are not interested in justice, they are interested in quiet.

Bill Cosby
(1937-) Comedian, Actor, Producer

No, you can't charge them rent while they're still in grade school.

Annie Pigeon
Present Day Writer

She was somewhere round eight when she planted both feet on the ground, crossed her arms, and told me that something I had done was not fair. I said that the world is not fair. She promptly replied, "Well, you don't have to add to it."

Beverly R. Silverberg
Present Day Lecturer, Author

My mom was fair. You never knew whether she was going to swing with her right hand or her left.

Herb Caen
(1916-1997) Pulitzer Prize-winning Columnist

PARENTHOOD

Insightful Observations on
PARENT-CHILD CONNECTION

Lucky parents who have fine children usually have lucky children who have fine parents.

James Brewer
20th Century Educator, Author

You don't really understand human nature unless you know why a child on a merry-go-round will wave at his parents every time around—and why his parents will always wave back.

William D. Tammeus
(1945-) Journalist, Author

When you're little, your life is UP, the future is UP; everything you want is UP—"wait-UP, hold-UP, shut-UP. Mom I'll clean UP, just let me stay UP." Parents are just the opposite, everything is DOWN—"Just calm DOWN, slow DOWN, come DOWN here, sit DOWN, put that DOWN."

Jerry Seinfeld
(1954-) Comedian, Actor, Producer

Worlds can be found by a child and adult bending down and looking together under the grass stems or at skittering crabs in a tidal pool.

Catherine Bateson
(1938-) Writer, Educator, Anthropologist

There's no trick to getting a kid to like you. Just feed him cookies and let him stay up past his bedtime.

J.F. Niel
Present Day Author

I understand the importance of bondage between parent and child.

Dan Quayle
(1947-) 44th U.S. Vice President

My mother and I could always look out the same window without ever seeing the same thing.

Gloria Swanson
(1897-1983) Actress, Producer

HAVING BABIES

CHILDHOOD

TEENAGERS

PARENTING

HOME LIFE

RELATIVES

PARENTHOOD

Insightful Observations on
LEADING BY EXAMPLE

Example is not the main thing in influencing others. It is the only thing.

 Albert Schweitzer
(1875-1965) Philosopher,
Physician, Humanitarian

I talk and talk and talk, and I haven't taught people in fifty years what my father taught me by example in one week.

 Mario Cuomo
(1932-) Former New York
Governor, Author

If you can't be a good example, then you'll just have to be a horrible warning.

 Catherine Aird
(1930-) British Writer

It's not only children who grow. Parents do too. As much as we watch to see what our children do with their lives, they are watching us to see what we do with ours. I can't tell my children to reach for the sun. All I can do is reach for it, myself.

Joyce Maynard
(1953-) Novelist, Political
Commentator

Children have never been very good at listening to their elders, but they have never failed to imitate them.

 James Baldwin
(1924-1987) Author

Setting a good example for your children takes all the fun out of middle age.

 William Feather
(1908-1976) Author

Don't try to make children grow up to be like you, or they may do it.

 Russell Baker
(1925-) Columnist, Humorist

170

PARENTHOOD

Insightful Observations on
OLDER PARENTS

No matter how old a mother is she watches her middle-aged children for signs of improvement.

> **Florida Scott-Maxwell**
> (1883-1979) Writer, Psychologist, Playwright

If only we could have them back as babies today, now that we know what to do with them.

> **Nancy Mairs**
> (1943-) Writer

Always be nice to your children because they are the ones who will choose your rest home.

> **Phyllis Diller**
> (1917-) Comedian, Actress, Author

As a mother, watching your children go off to start their own families is both heartening and hard. Now it's someone else who occupies first place in their lives, someone else they will call to say they've arrived safely. And they have suddenly become part of a whole new family tree; we are but one of their extended branches.

> **Cokie Roberts**
> (1943-) TV & Radio Journalist

Few things are more satisfying than seeing your own children have teenagers of their own.

> **Doug Larson**
> Present Day Cartoonist

My parents moved to Florida – they didn't want to, but they're in their sixties, and that's the law.

> **Jerry Seinfeld**
> (1954-) Comedian, Actor, Producer

Instead of saying hello, my mother gets on and says, "Guess who died?"

> **Dom Irrera**
> (1947-) Comedian, Actor, Writer

HAVING BABIES

CHILDHOOD

TEENAGERS

PARENTING

HOME LIFE

RELATIVES

PARENTHOOD

Insightful Observations on
TIME FOR YOURSELF

At night, when the house is quiet and the children have gone to sleep, I take a deep breath and listen to the steady beat of my heart.

 Jillian Karl
Present Day Author

So many women have chosen lives of seeming contradictions. I remember mentioning the babysitter in a column once and receiving outraged letters from readers who could not understand how anyone who could write feelingly of her children would hire help with their care. When did those people think I was writing? In the checkout line at the supermarket?

 Anna Quindlen
(1953-) Novelist, Social Critic, Columnist

From three to six months, most babies have settled down enough to be fun but aren't mobile enough to be getting into trouble. This is the time to pay some attention to your relationship again. Otherwise, you may spend the entire postpartum year thinking you married the wrong person and overlooking the obvious — that parenthood can create rough spots even in the smoothest marriage.

 Anne Cassidy
(1952-) Journalist, Author

I have two-year-old twins in my house, it's nuts. I make excuses to get out: "You need anything from anywhere? Anything from the Motor Vehicle Bureau? C'mon, let me register something. I was going out anyway, to apply for jury duty. Please!"

 Ray Romano
(1957-) Actor, Comedian

No day is so bad it can't be fixed with a nap.

 Author Unknown

172

PARENTHOOD

Insightful Observations on
SUCCEEDING
AS PARENTS

HAVING BABIES

CHILDHOOD

TEENAGERS

PARENTING

HOME LIFE

RELATIVES

I've got two wonderful children—and two out of five isn't bad.

Henny Youngman
(1906-1998) Comedian, Violinist

The best things you can give children, next to good habits, are good memories.

Sydney J. Harris
(1917-) American Journalist

If you want your children to turn out well, spend twice as much time on them and half as much money.

Abigail Van Buren
(1918-) Advice Columnist; Dear Abby

The Golden Rule of parenting is: Do unto your children as you wish your parents had done unto you!

Louise Hart
20th Century Psychologist, Author; The Winning Family

Your responsibility as a parent is not as great as you might imagine. You need not supply the world with the next conqueror of disease or major motion picture star. If your child simply grows up to be someone who does not use the word "collectible" as a noun, you can consider yourself an unqualified success.

Fran Lebowitz
(1950-) Writer, Humorist

A successful parent is one who raises a child who grows up and is able to pay for her own psychoanalysis.

Nora Ephron
(1941-) Writer, Director, Producer

 = IDEALIST = REALIST = CYNIC

173

HAVING BABIES

CHILDHOOD

TEENAGERS

PARENTING

HOME LIFE

RELATIVES

PARENTHOOD

Insightful Observations on
STEP-PARENTS

The role of the stepmother is the most difficult of all, because you can't ever just be. You're constantly being tested — by the children, the neighbors, your husband, the relatives, old friends who knew the children's parents in their first marriage, and by yourself.

 Anonymous Step-Parent

For even the most nurturing, devoted, loving stepfather has, with a step-daughter, an uphill battle. The relationship can test the mettle of the sturdiest marriage, the sanity of the most circumspect husband.

 Victoria Secunda
Present Day Psychologist, Author

From the adolescent's perspective, it's like discovering that another layer of management (the step-parent) is being thrust between you and the boss (parent) you've reported to for twelve, fourteen, or even sixteen years. Or worse, that the business (the home) has been bought out from under you. From the teenager's perspective, remarriage can feel like a hostile takeover.

 Laurence Steinberg
Present Day Professor of Psychology, Author

I am thinking about writing a play about bratty stepchildren. It is called, Not From My Vagina Monologues

Victoria Pearson
Present Day Stepmother;
referring to the hit play,
Vagina Monologues

174

PARENTHOOD

Insightful Observations on
GOD-PARENTS

HAVING BABIES

CHILDHOOD

TEENAGERS

PARENTING

HOME LIFE

RELATIVES

The modern role of the "God-Parent" is that of taking a vested interest in raising a more complete human being.

Oscar Herman
(1909-1980)
Humorist, Shoe Salesman

I'm a God-Mother—that's a great thing to be, a God-Mother. She calls me God for short. That's cute. I taught her that.

Ellen Degeneres
(1958-) Actor, Comedian, Talk Show Host

SENATOR KANE: Are you the son of Vito Corleone?
MICHAEL CORLEONE: Yes.
SENATOR KANE: Did he use, at times, an alias? Was this alias, in certain circles, GODFATHER?
MICHAEL CORLEONE: It was not an alias. GODFATHER was a term of affection, used by his friends, one of respect.

Al Pacino
in *The Godfather Part II* (1974)
written by Francis Ford Coppola & Mario Puzo

My goddaughter is so cute. She's two and a half. She saw her father in the shower and she came running out screaming, "Mommy, daddy has a tail!" Of course, I'm the evil single girl, I had to ask, "Is it a big tail?" Mommy's lucky.

Caroline Rhea
(1964-) Actor, Writer, Comedian

Always a God-Father—never a God.

Alexander Woollcott
(1887-1943) American Journalist, Drama Critic, Essayist

HAVING BABIES
CHILDHOOD
TEENAGERS
PARENTING
HOME LIFE
RELATIVES

FATHERHOOD

Insightful Observations on
BEING A FATHER

There is no more vital calling or vocation for men than fathering.

John R. Troop
20th Century Author

Sherman made the terrible discovery that men make about their fathers sooner or later... that the man before him was not an aging father but a boy, a boy much like himself, a boy who grew up and had a child of his own and, as best he could, out of a sense of duty and, perhaps love, adopted a role called Being a Father so that his child would have something mythical and infinitely important: a Protector, who would keep a lid on all the chaotic and catastrophic possibilities of life.

Tom Wolfe
(1931-) Author

Being a Father
Is quite a bother
You improve them mentally
And straighten them dentally,
They're no longer corralable
Once they find that you're fallible
But after you've raised them and educated them and gowned them,
They just take their little fingers and wrap you around them.
Being a Father
Is quite a bother,
But I like it, rather.

Ogden Nash
(1902-1971) Poet, Humorist

Being the father for triplets is like being the mother for one.

Josh Berman
(1969-) Entrepreneur,
Father of Triplets

Of a father of two there is a respectful question which I wish to ask a father of five: How do you happen to still be alive?

Ogden Nash
(1902-1971) Poet, Humorist

176

FATHERHOOD

Insightful Observations on
THE JOY OF FATHERHOOD

Some day you will know that a father is much happier in his children's happiness than his own. I cannot explain it to you: it is a feeling in your body that spreads gladness through you.

Honore De Balzac
(1799-1850) French Novelist

I don't ask much, do I? I mean I don't ask to be famous, and I don't ask to be rich, and I don't ask to play center field for the New York Yankees, or anything. I just want to meet a woman, and I want to fall in love, and I want to get married, and I want to have a kid, and I want to go see him play a tooth in the school play. It's not much.

Tom Hanks
in *Splash* (1984) written by Brian Grazer and Bruce Jay Friedman

Then I discovered that my son had learned something new. For the first time, he was able to give a proper kiss, puckering up his lips and enfolding my face in his arms. "Kees Dada," he said as he brushed me on the nose and cheeks. No amount of gratification at work could have compensated for that moment.

Donald H. Bell
20th Century Journalist

Once a relationship is underway, then I would say deafness would come in handy. Then once you're married and have kids, paralysis. "I'd love to drive you kids to that game, but I've got to sit in that chair and watch football on television.

Jerry Seinfeld
(1954-) Comedian, Actor, Producer

INSIGHTFUL OBSERVATIONS TO SHARE

177

HAVING BABIES

CHILDHOOD

TEENAGERS

PARENTING

HOME LIFE

RELATIVES

FATHERHOOD

Insightful Observations on FATHER'S ROLE

The most important thing a father can do for his children is to love their mother.

 Henry Ward Beecher
(1813-1887) Clergyman, Abolitionist

Anyone can be a father, but it takes a real man to be a dad.

 Author Unknown

Father, reading a magazine in an easy chair, speaks to son who stands next to him with a "Work Book" and a pencil: "Sorry, son. Daddy provides food, clothing, and shelter. The rest is up to you."

 Bernard Schoenbaum
Present Day Cartoonist in *The New Yorker*

Any man today who returns from work, sinks into a chair, and asks for his pipe is a man with an appetite for danger.

 Bill Cosby
(1937-) Comedian, Actor, Producer

What is it about American fathers as they grow older that makes them dress like flags from other countries?

 Cary Odes
Present Day Comedian, Actor

The place of the father in the modern suburban family is a very small one, particularly if he plays golf.

 Bertrand Russell
(1872-1970) Philosopher, Mathematician

FATHERHOOD

Insightful Observations on
FATHERS & DISCIPLINE

One father is more than a hundred Schoolmasters.

George Herbert
(1593-1633) Poet

RAY BARONE: All right Ally, you have to do what Mommy says.
ALLY BARONE: Why?
RAY BARONE: 'Cause I do.

Ray Romano
to Madylin Sweeten in
Everybody Loves Raymond
TV Sitcom

When I got about fourteen or fifteen, my Pops had to grab me and run me up against the wall one time just to let me know who was boss. I anticipate havin' to do mine the same way. Trust me, they'll have a better understanding of the world. Kids are always going to test their parents; it's natural. It's the parent who's got to pass the test.

Ice Cube
(1969-) Rapper, Actor, Composer

Father says to his two children: There are some words I will not tolerate in this house—and "awesome" is one of them.

Edward Koren
Present Day
Cartoonist in *The New Yorker*

Just wait until your father comes home!

Billions of Mothers Worldwide

😇 = IDEALIST   😊 = REALIST   🙂 = CYNIC

FATHERHOOD

Insightful Observations on
FATHERS ADVICE

My dad has always taught me these words: care and share.

Tiger Woods
(1975-) Professional Golfer

My father would say, "Do the best you can. And then the hell with it." He always looked at the effort grade rather than the final grade.

Ted Kennedy
(1932-) U.S. Senator From Massachusetts

My father taught me to always deliver more than you promise and you'll be surprised how opportunities open up for you.

Ted Giannoulas
Present Day Entertainer;
The San Diego Chicken

I remember being upset once and telling my dad I wasn't following through right. And he replied, "Nancy, it doesn't make a difference to a ball what you do after you hit it."

Nancy Lopez
(1957-) Professional Golfer

Poor Bush. He can't tell his daughters that if they waste their college years in drinking and partying, they'll never amount to anything.

Jay Leno
(1950-) Comedian, Talk show host

I'm a grown woman but my father still thinks I know nothing about my car. He always asks, "You changing the oil every 3,000?" "Yes, Dad. I'm also putting sugar in the gas tank. That way my exhaust smells like cotton candy."

Mimi Gonzalez
Present Day Actress
Comedian

My father said, "Mike, if you masturbate, you'll go blind." I said, "Dad—I'm over here."

Mike Binder
Present Day Actor,
Director, Writer

180

FATHERHOOD

Insightful Observations on
TYPES OF FATHERS

HAVING BABIES

CHILDHOOD

TEENAGERS

PARENTING

HOME LIFE

RELATIVES

What is it with dads? They turn forty or fifty and they become Mr. Fix It. You find 'em nude cruising around the house with a screwdriver in one hand. "I'm gonna tighten something."

Gary Barkin
Present Day Humorist,
Voice-over Actor

Something happens when a man reaches a certain age, that the News becomes the most important thing in his life. All fathers think one day they're going to get a call from the State Department. "Listen, we've completely lost track of the situation in the Middle East. You've been watching the news. What do you think we should do about it?"

Jerry Seinfeld
(1954-) Comedian, Actor,
Producer

My father listens to AM radio really loud. There's no reason for that.

Shashi Bhatia
Present Day Comedian,
Actor

Oh God, It's so hard for me and my father to understand each other. I mean, his favorite female artist is Celine Dion.

Madonna
(1958-) Singer, Songwriter,
Children's Book Author

My father was one of those people who went through life demanding to see the manager.

Oscar Herman
(1909-1980) Humorist, Shoe
Salesman

My father looked at kids as additions to his tool kit. He got me, apparently after thinking, "Oh, it's snowing again. I'll go back to bed and make a little snow-shoveling machine."

Bob Odenkirk
(1962-) Comedian, Actor,
Writer

WELLNESS THROUGH LAUGHTER

FATHERHOOD

Insightful Observations on
FATHERS & WORK

HAVING BABIES

CHILDHOOD

TEENAGERS

PARENTING

HOME LIFE

RELATIVES

I can run the country or control Alice. I can't do both.

 Theodore Roosevelt
(1858-1919) 26th U.S. President; **referring to his daughter**

Secretary seated at desk hands phone message to male executive: "Your daughter called—you promised to play phone tag with her today."

 Danny Shanahan
Present Day Cartoonist in *The New Yorker*

Stay-at-home dads are the frontline soldiers on an unforgiving battlefield, still fighting the expectations of what a dad's role in society is, and find, just like moms, the rewards are still worthwhile.

 Julian Orenstein
Present Day Writer, Columnist, Pediatrician

Before I had kids I went home after work to rest. Now I go to work to rest.

 Simon Ruddell
Present Day Author, Humorist

Commuter—one who spends his life
In riding to and from his wife;
A man who shaves and takes a train,
And then rides back to shave again.

 E.B. White
(1899-1985) Journalist, Author

FATHERHOOD

Insightful Observations on FATHER'S LOVE

Fathers are softer as they get older.

 Heather Locklear
(1961-) Actress

A man never stands as tall as when he kneels to help a child.

 Knights of Pythagoras
an organization composed of youths to aid youths

There's something like a line of gold thread running through a man's words when he talks to his daughter, and gradually, over the years, it gets to be long enough for you to pick up in your hands and weave into a cloth that feels like love itself.

 John Gregory Brown
20th Century Novelist

You don't have to deserve your mother's love. You have to deserve your father's. He is more particular... The father is always a Republican towards his son, and his mother's always a Democrat.

 Robert Frost
(1874-1963) Poet

After watching the Kevorkian trial, I asked my father, "Do you think family should have the right to withdraw life support on a loved one?" He said, "It depends on which kid."

 Hugh Fink
Present Day Comedian, Writer, Actor

BART: Dad, I can't believe you're risking my life to save your own!
HOMER: Son, you'll understand one day, when you have kids.

 The Simpsons
Animated TV Series

INSIGHTFUL OBSERVATIONS TO SHARE

183

FATHERHOOD

Insightful Observations on
FATHERS & DAUGHTERS

The only man a girl can depend on is her daddy.

Grease
(1978) Musical by Jim Jacobs and Warren Casey, Screenplay by Allan Carr

Old as she was, she still missed her daddy sometimes.

Gloria Naylor
(1950-) Author

The meaningful role of the father of the bride was played out long before the church music began. It stretched across those years of infancy and puberty, adolescence and young adulthood. That's when she needs you at her side.

Tom Brokaw
(1940-) Broadcast Journalist

The father of a daughter is nothing but a high-class hostage. A father turns a stony face to his sons, berates them, shakes his antlers, paws the ground, snorts, runs them off into the underbrush, but when his daughter puts her arm over his shoulder and says, "Daddy, I need to ask you something," he is a pat of butter in a hot frying pan.

Garrison Keillor
(1942-) Radio Host, Writer

You mustn't get aggravated when your old dad calls you his baby, because he always will think of you as just that—no matter how old or big you may get.

Harry S. Truman
(1884-1972) 33rd U.S. President; **to his daughter, Margaret**

A father is always making his baby into a little woman. And when she is a woman he turns her back again.

Enid Bagnold
(1889-1981) Novelist, Playwright

184

FATHERHOOD

Insightful Observations on
FATHERS & SONS

My father used to play with my brother and me in the yard. Mother would come out and say, "You're tearing up the grass." "We're not raising grass," Dad would reply. "We're raising boys."

Harmon Killebrew
(1936-) Professional
Baseball Player

When I was a boy of fourteen, my father was so ignorant I could hardly stand to have the old man around. But when I got to be twenty-one, I was astonished at how much the old man had learned in seven years.

Mark Twain
(1835-1910) Writer, Humorist

I didn't hire Scott as an assistant coach because he's my son. I hired him because I'm married to his mother.

Frank Layden
20th Century Basketball
Coach

I distrust any man who claims to have had a continuous friendship with his father. How did he get from fourteen to twenty-six?

Verlyn Klinkenborg
Author, Editor, Journalist

By the time a man realizes that maybe his father was right, he usually has a son who thinks he's wrong.

Charles Wadsworth
(1929-) Musician

FATHER TO SON: When Abe Lincoln was your age, he walked ten miles to school, split logs, and studied by candlelight.
SON: When John Kennedy was your age, he was President.

Author Unknown

I never got along with my dad. Kids used to come up to me and say, "My dad can beat up your dad." I'd say, "Yeah? When?"

Bill Hicks
(1961-1994) Comedian

😄 = IDEALIST   😊 = REALIST   🙂 = CYNIC

185

HAVING BABIES

CHILDHOOD

TEENAGERS

PARENTING

HOME LIFE

RELATIVES

HAVING BABIES

CHILDHOOD

TEENAGERS

PARENTING

HOME LIFE

RELATIVES

FATHERHOOD

Insightful Observations on
ENDING UP
LIKE YOUR FATHER

I don't mind looking in the mirror and seeing my father.

Michael Douglas
(1944-) Actor, Producer

Like father, like son.

Proverb

My father was a statesman, I'm a political woman. My father was a saint. I'm not.

Indira Gandhi
(1900-1984) First Female Prime Minister of India

My son has a new nickname for me, "Baldy." Son, I've got a new word for you, "Heredity."

Dan Savage
Sex-Advice Columnist

You can't compare me to my father. Our similarities are different.

Dale Berra
(1956-) Son of Yogi Berra
(1925-) Baseball Player, Coach

I grew up to have my father's looks, my father's speech patterns, my father's posture, my father's walk, my father's opinions and my mothers contempt for my father.

Jules Feiffer
(1929-) Cartoonist, Playwright

For rarely are sons similar to their fathers: most are worse, and a few are better than their fathers.

Homer
(7th Century BC) Greek Poet; *The Odyssey*

186

MOTHERHOOD

Insightful Observations on
BEING A MOTHER

HAVING BABIES

CHILDHOOD

TEENAGERS

PARENTING

HOME LIFE

RELATIVES

Biology is the least of what makes someone a mother.

 Oprah Winfrey
(1954-) TV Talk Show Host, Actress, Humanitarian

It's the biggest on-the-job training program in existence today.

 Erma Bombeck
(1927-1996) Humorist, Author

There's a lot more to being a woman than being a mother, but there's a hell of a lot more to being a mother than most people suspect.

 Roseanne Barr
(1952-) Actress, Comedian, Talk Show Host, Producer

Being constantly with children was like wearing a pair of shoes that were expensive and too small. She couldn't bear to throw them out, but they gave her blisters.

 Beryl Bainbridge
(1934-) British Writer

Motherhood is the second oldest profession in the world. It never questions age, height, religious preference, health, political affiliation, citizenship, morality, ethnic background, marital status, economic level, convenience, or previous experience.

Erma Bombeck
(1927-1996) Humorist, Author

Men and children. . . think that if you're sitting down it means you're waiting for someone to give you something to do.

 Serena Gray
20th Century Author

Q: What would have made a family and career easier for you?
A: Being born a man.

 Anonymous Mother

HAVING BABIES

CHILDHOOD

TEENAGERS

PARENTING

HOME LIFE

RELATIVES

MOTHERHOOD

Insightful Observations on
THE JOY OF MOTHERHOOD

Nothing else will ever make you as happy or as sad, as proud or as tired, as Motherhood

 Ella Parsons
Present Day Author; *The Mother's Almanac*

.

Nothing else ever will make you as happy or as sad, as proud or as tired, for nothing is quite as hard as helping a person develop his own individuality—especially while you struggle to keep your own.

 Marguerite Kelly and Elia Parsons
Present Day Authors

It is certainly not new or startling to find that women feel the desire to take care of their children. What is new is the number of women who are startled by such feelings.

 Elaine Heffner
20th Century Psychiatrist
Author; *Mothering*

I was often bewildered by the task of motherhood, that precarious balance between total surrender and totalitarianism.

 J. Nozipo Maraire
(1966-) African Novelist

A mother is someone who looks forward to getting a root canal so she can sit quietly in one place.

 Beth Mende
Present Day Comedian

188

MOTHERHOOD

Insightful Observations on
MOTHERS & STRESS

HAVING BABIES

CHILDHOOD

TEENAGERS

PARENTING

HOME LIFE

RELATIVES

A mother is like a tea bag—only in hot water do you realize how strong she is.

Nancy Reagan
(1921-) Wife of 40th U.S. President Ronald Reagan

Any mother could perform the jobs of several air traffic controllers with ease.

Lisa Alther
(1944-) Writer

A woman who can cope with the terrible twos can cope with anything.

Judith Clabes
(1945-) Teacher, Journalist, CEO

With two sons born eighteen months apart, I operated mainly on automatic pilot through the ceaseless activity of their early childhood. I remember opening the refrigerator late one night and finding a roll of aluminum foil next to a pair of small red tennis shoes. Certain that I was responsible for the refrigerated shoes, I quickly closed the door and ran upstairs to make sure I had put the babies in their cribs instead of the linen closet.

Mary Kay Blakeley
Present Day Journalist, Author; *American Mom*

In some ways you go through motherhood in an under-siege mentality. You never admit how hard things are till they're safely behind you.

Liz Rosenberg
(1958-) Educator, Poet, Author

You get a lot of tension. You get a lot of headaches. I do what it says on the aspirin bottle: Take two and keep away from children.

Roseanne Barr
(1952-) Actress, Comedian, Talk Show Host, Producer

MOTHERHOOD

Insightful Observations on MOTHER'S ROLE

God could not be everywhere and therefore he made mothers.

Jewish Proverb

Mothers have as powerful an influence over the welfare of future generations as all other causes combined.

John Abbott
(1805-1877) British Author

A mother! What are we worth really? They all grow up whether you look after them or not.

Christina Stead
(1902-1983) Australian Writer

Is it really asking too much of a woman to expect her to bring up her husband and her children, too?

Lillian Bell
20th Century Author

Hey, the way I figure it is this: if the kids are still alive by the time my husband comes home, I've done my job

Roseanne Barr
(1952-) Actress, Comedian, Talk Show Host, Producer

A woman knows all about her children. She knows about dentist appointments and soccer games and romances and best friends and favorite foods and secret fears and hopes and dreams. A man is vaguely aware of some short people living in the house.

Matt Groening
(1954-) Writer, Humorist, Cartoonist

I think it's a mother's duty to embarrass her children.

Cher
(1946-) Actress, Singer, Director

THE GUIDE TO LAUGHING AT FAMILY

MOTHERHOOD

Insightful Observations on
TYPES OF MOTHERS

HAVING BABIES

CHILDHOOD

TEENAGERS

PARENTING

HOME LIFE

RELATIVES

I am not a cookie-baking mother. Well, that's not true. I am a cookie-baking mother, but I am not a traditional cookie-baking mother.

 Cher
(1946-) Actress, Singer, Director

The myth of superwoman has hung on long after the media stopped airing fantasy-based commercials about working women's lives: here she comes, home from the office after 12 hours of high-powered negotiations in the executive suite. Her designer suit is still fresh and unwrinkled, her face radiant and unlined as she opens her arms to greet her two adorable children—and sends a seductive glance toward her handsome husband, beaming proudly in the background. Watch her as, with one smooth motion, she slips off her jacket and into a dainty apron as she glides toward the spotless kitchen to create a three-course meal for her beloved family. After dinner she will check the children's French homework and read them a chapter of Jane Eyre before tucking the little cherubs into bed. While her husband watches the late-night news, she will disappear into the den to make an overseas call that will clinch a multimillion dollar deal for her company.

 Deborah Swiss
Present Day Educator, Author; *Women and the Work Family Dilemma*

My mom's your typical suburban Hindu. Just picture Donna Reed with a dot.

 Shashi Bhatia
Present Day Comedian, Actor

My mother had a problem because she grew up during the Great Depression. And I had problems because I grew up during her great depression.

 Jane Stroll
Present Day Comedian, Actor

 = IDEALIST   = REALIST   = CYNIC

MOTHERHOOD

Insightful Observations on
MOTHER SKILLS

I know how to do anything—I'm a mom.

 Roseane Barr
(1952-) Comedian, TV Talk
Show Host, Actor, Producer

Mom will clean up everything. Scientists have proven that a mom's spit is the exact chemical composition of Formula 409. Mom's spit on a Kleenex: You get rust off a bumper with that thing.

 Jeff Foxworthy
(1958-) Comedian, Actor

Motherhood in all its guises and permutations is more art than science.

 Melinda M. Marshall
Present Day Author,
Educator

Perhaps nobody becomes more competent in hitting a moving target than a mother spoon feeding a baby.

 Author Unknown

Now, as always, the most automated appliance in a household is the mother.

 Beverly Jones
(1927-) Writer, Feminist

I don't know why no one ever thought to paste a label on the toilet-tissue spindle giving 1-2-3 directions for replacing the tissue on it. Then everyone in the house would know what Mama knows.

 Erma Bombeck
(1927-1996) Humorist, Author

If evolution really works, how come mothers only have two hands?

 Milton Berle
(1908-2002) Comedian,
Actor, TV Personality

MOTHERHOOD

Insightful Observations on
MOTHER'S SACRIFICE

HAVING BABIES

CHILDHOOD

TEENAGERS

PARENTING

HOME LIFE

RELATIVES

A mother is a person who seeing there are only four pieces of pie for five people, promptly announces she never did care for pie.

 Tenneva Jordan
20th Century Author

Motherhood meant I have written four fewer books, but I know more about life.

 A.S. Byatt
(1936-) British Author

When you are a mother, you are never really alone in your thoughts. A mother always has to think twice, once for herself and once for her child.

 Sophia Loren
(1934-) Actress, Sex Symbol

A man's work is from sun to sun, but a mother's work is never done.

Author Unknown

The mother of three notoriously unruly youngsters was asked whether or not she'd have children if she had to do over again. "Sure," she replied, "but not the same ones."

Author Unknown

I love my kids, but I need something more. Like, perhaps, a life.

 Roseanne Barr
in TV Show *Roseanne* (1988-1997)

It's not easy being a mother. If it were easy, fathers would do it.

 Beatrice Arthur
as Dorothy in *The Golden Girls* TV Show (1985-1992)

193

HAVING BABIES

CHILDHOOD

TEENAGERS

PARENTING

HOME LIFE

RELATIVES

MOTHERHOOD

Insightful Observations on
MOTHER'S LOVE

Do you have any idea how much I love you?

 All Mothers

The greatest love is a mother's , then a dog's, then a sweetheart's

 Polish Proverb

Mother love is the fuel that enables a normal human being to do the impossible.

 Marion C. Garretty
20th century Author

I am not a classic mother. But my kids were never palmed off to boarding school. So I didn't bake cookies. You can buy cookies, but you can't buy love.

 Rachel Welch
(1940-) Actress, Sex Symbol

This is the reason why mothers are more devoted to their children than fathers: it is that they suffer more in giving them birth and are more certain that they are their own.

 Aristotle
(384-322 B.C.) Greek
Philospher, Scientist

The mother-child relationship is paradoxical and, in a sense, tragic. It requires the most intense love on the mother's side, yet this very love must help the child grow away from the mother and to become fully independent.

 Erich Fromm
(1900-1980) Psychologist,
Philosopher

When I was a boy, my mother wore a mood ring. Whenever she was in a good mood, it turned blue. Whenever she was in a bad mood, it left a big red mark in the middle of my forehead.

 Jeff Shaw
(1966-) Comedian

Nobody loves me like my mother and she could be jivin' too.

 BB King
(1925-) Blues Musician

THE GUIDE TO LAUGHING AT FAMIL

MOTHERHOOD

Insightful Observations on
MOTHERS & DAUGHTERS

HAVING BABIES

CHILDHOOD

TEENAGERS

PARENTING

HOME LIFE

RELATIVES

My daughters enlighten me about myself. Their presence acts as a constant, ever-changing reflection of me as well as a source of feedback, as I see myself mirrored in their mannerisms, attitudes and relationships.

Ellen A. Rosen
Present Day Author

A daughter is a mother's gender partner, her closest ally in the family confederacy, an extension of her self. And mothers are their daughters' role model, their biological and emotional road map, the arbiter of all their relationships.

Victoria Secunda
Present Day Psychologist, Author

All daughters, even when most aggravated by their mothers, have a secret respect for them.

Phyllis Bottoms
Present Day Author

Of all the haunting moments of motherhood, few rank with hearing your own words come out of your daughter's mouth.

Victoria Secunda
Present Day Psychologist, Author

It's weird that I have a parent who's a shrink. It's hard to think of my mom solving other people's problems when she's the root of all mine.

Carol Leifer
(1956-) Comedian, Writer, Actress, Producer

HAVING BABIES

CHILDHOOD

TEENAGERS

PARENTING

HOME LIFE

RELATIVES

MOTHERHOOD

Insightful Observations on
MOTHERS & SONS

For a woman, a son offers the best chance to know the mysteries of male existence.

 Carole Klein
Present Day Author;
Mothers and Sons

If you are going to kill each other, do it outside...I just finished cleaning!

 Anonymous Mother

I love being a mom. My four year old son tells me how pretty I am, that he loves me and wants to marry me. I love him too, but I don't think he could support me in the style to which I'm accustomed. Not as a Power Ranger, anyway.

 Liz Sells
Present Day Comedian

Never marry a man who hates his mother, because he will end up hating you.

 Jill Bennett
(1920-1990) Actress

Mothers tend to encourage their sons to runaway and romp... Mothers of little boys often complain that "There's no controlling him. He's all over the place..." The complaints are tinged with more than a little pride at the boy's marvelous independence and masculine bravado. It's almost as though the mother enjoyed being overwhelmed by her spectacular conquering hero.

Louise J. Kaplan
20th Century Psychologist
Author

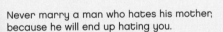

The greatest battle that was ever fought-
Shall I tell you where and when?
On the maps of the world you will find it not:
It was fought by mothers of men.

 Joaquin Miller
(1837-1913) Poet

Most men are secretly mad at their mothers for throwing away their comic books. They would be valuable now.

 Rita Rudner
(1956-) Comedian

MOTHERHOOD

Insightful Observations on
WORKING MOTHERS

HAVING BABIES

CHILDHOOD

TEENAGERS

PARENTING

HOME LIFE

RELATIVES

All mothers are working mothers.

 Modern proverb

I have a brain and a uterus and I use them both.

 Patricia Schroeder
(1940-) Congresswoman; **on being asked how she could be both a congresswoman and a mother**

Being asked to decide between your passion for work or your passion for children was like being asked by your doctor whether you preferred him to remove your brain or your heart.

 Mary Kay Blakely
Present Day Journalist, Author

I did not fear being able to work again so much as never wanting to work again.

 Jane Lazarre
Present Day Author

At work, you think of the children you've left at home. At home, you think of the work you've left unfinished.

 Golda Meir
(1898-1978) Israeli Prime Minister

I think we're seeing in working mothers a change from "Thank God it's Friday" to "Thank God it's Monday."

 Anne Diehl
Present Day Actor, Director, Author

After decades of unappreciated drudgery, American women just don't do housework anymore—that is, beyond the minimum that is required in order to clear a path from the bedroom to the front door so they can get off to work in the morning.

 Barbara Ehrenreich
(1941-) Essayist, Author

 = IDEALIST   = REALIST 😐 = CYNIC

197

MOTHERHOOD

Insightful Observations on
FULL-TIME MOTHERS

I don't like the terms housewife and homemaker. I prefer to be called Domestic Goddess...it's more descriptive.

 Roseanne Barr
(1952-) Actress, Comedian, Talk Show Host, Producer

Being a full-time mother is one of the highest salaried jobs...since the payment is pure love.

 Mildred B. Vermont
20th Century Author

If the women's movement did any harm at all, it gave the women who stayed at home an inferiority complex.

Barbara Walters
(1931-) News Correspondent, Producer

By and large, mothers and housewives are the only workers who do not have regular time off. They are the great vacationless class.

Anne Morrow Lindbergh
(1906-2001) Author; Pilot; wife of Charles A. Lindbergh

I prefer the word "homemaker" because "housewife" always implies that there may be a wife someplace else.

 Bella Abzug
(1920-1998) Actress, Civil Rights Activist

MOTHERHOOD

Insightful Observations on
SINGLE MOTHERS

HAVING BABIES

CHILDHOOD

TEENAGERS

PARENTING

HOME LIFE

RELATIVES

I have a lot of friends who are bringing up their children alone. Men are not a necessity. You don't need them to live. You don't have to have them to survive.

 Cher
(1946-) Actress, Singer, Director

I'm a single mother. When I say that I say it with Pride, Humility, Fear, Gratefulness and Honor. Kind of an odd mixture of feelings, wouldn't you say?

Kathleen Driggers
Present Day Singe Mom, Entrepreneur

When you have a good mother and no father, God kind of sits in. It's not enough, but it helps.

 Dick Gregory
(1932-) Actor, Comedian, Activist

I was reading how a female spider will eat the male spider after mating. I guess female spiders know that life insurance is easier to collect than child support.

Janine DiTullio
Present Day Comedian, Actress, Writer

It's all any reasonable child can expect if the dad is present at the conception.

 Joe Orton
(1933-1967) British Dramatist

"Single Mother" is a polite way of saying, "broke, exhausted, and nobody will date your ass."

 John Leguizamo
(1964-) Actor, Writer

HAVING BABIES

CHILDHOOD

TEENAGERS

PARENTING

HOME LIFE

RELATIVES

MOTHERHOOD

Insightful Observations on
ENDING UP
LIKE YOUR MOTHER

As is the mother, so is her daughter.

 The Bible: Ezekiel

Sooner or later we all quote our mothers.

 Bern Williams
Present Day Author

Women can never quite escape their mothers' cosmic pull, not their lip-biting expectations or their faulty love. We want to please our mothers, emulate them, disgrace them, oblige them, outrage them, and bury ourselves in the mysteries and consolations of their presence.

 Carol Shields
(1935-2003) University Professor, Author

Nearly every day an echo of my mother's mothering wafts by me, like the aroma of soup simmering on a stove down the street.

.

 Anna Quindlen
(1953-) Novelist, Social Critic, Columnist

All women become like their mothers. That is their tragedy. No man does. That's his.

 Oscar Wilde
(1854-1900) Poet, Playwright, Novelist

200

Insightful Observations

HAVING BABIES

CHILDHOOD

TEENAGERS

PARENTING

HOME LIFE

RELATIVES

Step Five:

HO
L

ME
FE

The Family
The Home
Money
Family Gatherings

HAVING BABIES

CHILDHOOD

TEENAGERS

PARENTING

HOME LIFE

RELATIVES

THE FAMILY

Insightful Observations on
THE FAMILY UNIT

The family, that dear octopus from whose tentacles we never quite escape, nor in our innermost hearts ever quite wish to.

 Dodie Smith
(1896-1990) Writer

Soup is a lot like a family. Each ingredient enhances the others; each batch has its own characteristics; and it needs time to simmer to reach full flavor.

 Marge Kennedy
Present Day Author

Family is just an accident. They don't mean to get on your nerves. They don't even mean to be in your family, they just are.

 Marsha Norman
(1947-) Stage & Screenwriter

The household is a choreography of large and small mammals pursuing their own cross purposes.

 Mary Catherine Bateson
(1939-) Writer, Cultural Anthropologist

CARRIE: Wallis was right. The most important thing in life is your family. There are days you love them, and others you don't, but in the end, they're the people you always come home to. Sometimes it's the family you're born into and sometimes it's the one you make for yourself.

 Sarah Jessica Parker
in HBO's *Sex and the City*

A family is a unit composed not only of children but of men, women, an occasional animal, and the common cold.

 Ogden Nash
(1902-1971) Poet, Humorist

204

THE FAMILY

Insightful Observations on
GETTING ALONG WITH FAMILY

I think that husbands and wives should live in separate houses. If there's enough money, the children should live in a third.

 Cloris Leachman
(1926-) Actor

I get along great with my parents. I still talk to them at least once a week. It's the least I can do. I still live in their house.

 David Corrado
Present Day Humorist

Family Life! The United Nations is child's play compared to the tugs and splits and need to understand and forgive in any family.

 May Sarton
(1912-1995) Belgian-American Poet, Novelist

I am the person most qualified to host a talk show. I have five kids from three different marriages; my sister and brother are gay; I have multiple personalities; and the National Enquirer reunited me with my daughter.

 Roseanne Barr
(1952-) Actress, Comedian, Talk Show Host, Producer

MALCOLM: That's the way discussions go down in this family. I tell them my needs, and they say no. Then dad reveals another cartoon character he's afraid of.

 Frankie Muniz
in *Malcolm in the Middle* TV Sitcom

Often the reason we cannot get along with our families is because they are like a mirror in which we see our own faults in all their hideousness.

 Dorothy Dix
(1870-1951) Journalist, Writer

 = IDEALIST   = REALIST   = CYNIC

HAVING BABIES

CHILDHOOD

TEENAGERS

PARENTING

HOME LIFE

RELATIVES

THE FAMILY

Insightful Observations on

FAMILY COMMUNICATION

Stop yelling. If you want to ask me something, come here. STOP YELLING. IF YOU WANT TO ASK ME SOMETHING, COME HERE.

 Delia Ephron
Present Day Writer, Producer

One important reason to stay calm is that calm parents hear more. Low-key, accepting parents are the ones whose kids keep talking.

 Mary Pipher
20th Century Psychologist, Author

My mother never saw the irony in calling me a son-of-a-bitch.

 Jack Nicholson
(1937-) Actor

We never talked in our family. We communicated by putting Ann Landers articles on the fridge.

 Judy Gold
Present Day Comedian, Writer

Women speak because they wish to speak, whereas a man speaks only when driven to speech by something outside of himself, like, for instance, he can't find clean socks.

Jean Kerr
(1922-2003) Writer, Dramatist, Lyricist

One of my more effective parental strategies is to make Lists of Rules to be Obeyed And I Really Mean it This Time, and post these articles on the refrigerator in the kitchen so my children will have a written record of what they are ignoring.

 Bruce Cameron
(1919-1959) Actor, Writer

I had written to Aunt Maud,
Who was on a trip abroad,
When I heard she'd died of cramp
Just too late to save the stamp.

 Harry Graham
(1929-) Suspense Novelist

THE GUIDE TO LAUGHING AT FAMILY

THE FAMILY

Insightful Observations on
DYSFUNCTIONAL FAMILIES

HAVING BABIES

CHILDHOOD

TEENAGERS

PARENTING

HOME LIFE

RELATIVES

Well, as I always say, a family of freaks is better than no family at all.

 Family Guy
Animated TV Show (1999-2002)

My family is so dysfunctional that if I had to write a song about them, it would be called, Gimme, Ain't You Got, Loan Me, Don't You Have. It would be No.1 on the country-western charts for weeks.

 Paulara R. Hawkins
Present Day Comedian, Actress

I think a dysfunctional family is any family with more than one person in it.

 May Karr
(1955-) Author

All happy families resemble one another, each unhappy family is unhappy in its own way.

 Leo Tolstoy
(1828-1910) Russian Writer

Nobody's family can hang out the sign, "Nothing the matter here."

 Chinese Proverb

I come from a typical American family. You know, me, my mother, her third husband, his daughter from a second marriage, my step-sister, her illegitimate son.

 Carol Henry
(1918-1987) Actor, Writer

My ex-wife's family was crazy. I read an article on dysfunctional families, and it opened my eyes. I realized it would take them years of therapy just to work their way up to dysfunctional. Their family coat of arms was a biohazard symbol on a field of empty beer cans.

 Daniel Liebert
Present Day Comedian

THE FAMILY

Insightful Observations on FAMILY SANITY

When we remember we are all mad, the mysteries disappear and life stands explained.

Mark Twain
(1835-1910) Writer, Humorist

Never, EVER serve sugary snacks on rainy days.

Author Unknown

My mom has her own psychological problems. We just had to enroll her in Shoulder Pads Anonymous.

Stephanie Schiern
Present Day Comedian

Families are like fudge… mostly sweet with a few nuts.

Author Unknown

The home is ruled by the sickest person in it.

Nitzberg's Observation

When I became a father, I learned that insanity in children, like radio transmissions, is liveliest at night.

Bill Cosby
(1937-) Comedian, Actor, Producer

Insanity is hereditary; you get it from your children.

Sam Levenson
(1911-1980) Humorist, Author

Insanity runs in my family. It practically gallops.

Cary Grant
(1904-1986) Actor

208

HAVING BABIES

CHILDHOOD

TEENAGERS

PARENTING

HOME LIFE

RELATIVES

THE FAMILY

Insightful Observations on FAMILY THERAPY

HAVING BABIES

CHILDHOOD

TEENAGERS

PARENTING

HOME LIFE

RELATIVES

A Freudian slip is when you say one thing but mean your mother.

 Author Unknown

In my family, everyone is seeing a psychologist, except my mother. She creates the patients.

 Stephanie Schiern
Present Day Comedian

Have you ever been in therapy? No? You should try it. It's like a really easy gameshow where the correct answer to every question is: "Because of my mother."

 Robin Greenspan
20th Century Musician

Don't join encounter groups. If you enjoy being made to feel inadequate, call your mother.

 Liz Smith
(1923-) Gossip Columnist

I've been in therapy once a week for sixteen years. My friend thought that was rather extensive, so I brought her home to meet my family. Now she goes twice a week.

 Cathy Ladman
(1955-) Comedian

My mom had the breakdown for the family, and I went to therapy for all of us.

 Carrie Fisher
(1956-) Actress, Writer

We're supposed to take our problems to a family advisor. Personally, I've never met a family advisor. They're all off somewhere listening to dirty stories.

 Robert Orben
(1927-) Author, Humorist

INSIGHTFUL OBSERVATIONS TO SHARE

THE FAMILY

Insightful Observations on FAMILY TREES

I am my own ancestor.

Duc d'Abrantes
(1771-1813) French General

Never brag about your ancestors coming over on the Mayflower—the immigration laws weren't as strict in those days.

Lew Lehr
(1895-1950) Editor, Screenwriter

I don't know who my grandfather was; I am much more concerned to know what his grandson will be.

Abraham Lincoln
(1809-1865) 16th US President

If your family tree does not fork, you might be a redneck.

Jeff Foxworthy
(1958-) Comedian, Actor, Writer

My family tree was chopped down and they made the lumber into toilet paper. We've never been closer.

Barry Steiger
Present Day Comedian, Actor

I don't have to look up my family tree, because I know that I'm the sap.

Fred Allen
(1894-1956) Comedian, Radio Personality

Some family trees are more of a bush.

Author Unknown

THE FAMILY

Insightful Observations on FAMILY SKELETONS

HAVING BABIES

CHILDHOOD

TEENAGERS

PARENTING

HOME LIFE

RELATIVES

If you cannot get rid of the family skeleton, you may as well make it dance.

 George Bernard Shaw
(1856-1950) Playwright, Novelist, Critic

He comes from a rich family—his brother is worth $50,000 dead or alive.

 Author Unknown

Family jokes, though rightly cursed by strangers, are the bond that keeps most families intact.

 Stella Benson
(1892-1933) British Novelist

There is something about a closet that makes a skeleton restless.

 Author Unknown

It's a family that's loaded with grudges and passion. We come from a long line of robbers and highwaymen in Italy, you know. Killers, even.

 Nicholas Cage
(1964-) Actor; **on his family, the Coppallas**

When Daddy and Mum got quite plastered, And their shame had been thoroughly mastered, They told their boy, Harry: 'Son, we never did marry. But don't tell the neighbors, you bastard.'

 Author Unknown

Descended from Apes? My dear, we hope that it is not true. But if it is, let us pray that it may not become generally known.

 Author Unknown

 = IDEALIST    = REALIST   = CYNIC

211

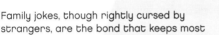

HAVING BABIES

CHILDHOOD

TEENAGERS

PARENTING

HOME LIFE

RELATIVES

THE FAMILY

Insightful Observations on
WHERE YOU'RE FROM

SNOBBISH WOMAN: Why on earth were you ever born in such an unfashionable place as Lowell, Massachusetts?
JAMES WHISTLER: I wanted to be nearer my mother.

James Whistler
(1834-1903) Painter

The family you come from isn't as important as the family you're going to have.

Ring Lardner
(1885-1933) Journalist, Writer

There is no Shah who has not had a slave among his ancestors and no slave who has not had a Shah among his. Never be ashamed of who you are.

Mansoor Shah
(1926-) Pakistan Air Force Comander, Writer

Suburbia: where they tear out the trees and then name streets after them.

Author Unknown

I grew up on Long Island. People always ask me if I come from money. I actually come from coupons.

Wendy Liebman
(1961-) Comedian

I come from a small town whose population never changed. Each time a woman got pregnant someone left town.

Michael Prichard
Present Day Actor, Writer, Comedian

The town where I grew up has a zip code of E-I-E-I-O.

Martin Mull
(1943-) Actor, Producer, Writer, Comedian

THE GUIDE TO LAUGHING AT FAMILY

THE FAMILY

Insightful Observations on
ROYAL FAMILIES

You are a member of the British royal family. We are never tired, and we all love hospitals.

Queen Mary
(1867-1953) Wife of George V; **to her daughter, Queen Elizabeth II**

Like all the best families, we have our share of eccentricities, of impetuous and wayward youngsters and of family disagreements.

Queen Elizabeth II
(1926-) Queen of England

They are not royal, they just happen to have me as their aunt.

Queen Elizabeth II
(1926-) Queen of England; **about Princess Margaret's children**

My father was frightened of his mother. I was frightened of my father, and I'm damned well going to make sure that my children are frightened of me.

George V
(1865-1936) King of England

George the Third,
Ought never to have occurred.
One can only wonder,
At so grotesque a blunder.

E.C. Bentley
(1875-1956) Journalist, Novelist, Poet

The difference between us is that my family begins with me, whereas yours ends with you.

Iphicrates
(415-353 BC) Athenian General; **reply to a descendant of Harmodius (an Athenian hero) who had derided Iphicrates for being the son of a cobbler**

213

HAVING BABIES

CHILDHOOD

TEENAGERS

PARENTING

HOME LIFE

RELATIVES

THE FAMILY

Insightful Observations on
YOUNGER GENERATIONS

There is no finer investment for any community than putting milk into babies.

 Winston Churchill
(1874-1965) British Statesman

It is easier to build strong children than to repair broken men.

 Frederick Douglass
(1817-1895) Black Author, Human Rights Leader

One day, a girl walked up to her mother and looked at her mother's hair and sadly said: "Mom, why is some of your hair white?" The mother replied, "Well, every time that you do something wrong and make me cry or unhappy, one of my hairs turns white." The girl thought about this revelation a while, and then said, "Mom, how come all of grandma's hairs are white?"

 Author Unknown

They've grown up and moved to Minneapolis. Every generation goes someplace bigger.

 Faith Sullivan
Present Day Author

Parents often talk about the younger generation as if they didn't have anything to do with it.

 Haim Ginott
(1922-1972) Israeli Child Psychologist

When you teach your son, you teach your son's son.

 The Talmud

214

THE FAMILY

Insightful Observations on
HEREDITY

There is nothing like having grandchildren to restore your faith in heredity.

 Doug Larson
Present Day Cartoonist

I want you to know how I feel about my Italian heritage, so I'd like to say a few words in Italian: Verdi, Pavarotti, DiMaggio, Valentino, Giuliani...

 Susan Lucci
(1947-) Actress

Important families are like potatoes. The best parts are underground.

 Francis Bacon
(1909-1992) Designer,
Painter

If your parents never had children, chances are you won't, either.

 Dick Cavett
(1936-) TV Talk Show Host

Nothing is so soothing to our self-esteem as to find our bad traits in our forebears. It seems to absolve us.

 Van Wyck Brooks
(1886-1963) Literary Critic,
Historian

Heredity is what sets the parents of a teenager wondering about each other.

 Laurence J. Peter
(1919-1988) Writer, Educator

HAVING BABIES

CHILDHOOD

TEENAGERS

PARENTING

HOME LIFE

RELATIVES

INSIGHTFUL OBSERVATIONS TO SHARE

HAVING BABIES

CHILDHOOD

TEENAGERS

PARENTING

HOME LIFE

RELATIVES

THE FAMILY

Insightful Observations on

FAMILY
VALUES & MORALS

My parents are what you would call "old world." They're very stable, down-to-earth people. They don't believe in divorce. Their values are God and carpeting.

Woody Allen
(1935-) Writer, Actor, Director

Father in swimming pool at lavish mansion talking to son: "Someday, son, all this and more will be yours if you remember to always support the Republican party."

Edward Frascino
Present Day Cartoonist in *The New Yorker*

Bedding is important. So are hair products.

Heather Locklear
(1961-) Actress

To educate a person in mind and not in morals is to educate a menace to society.

Theodore Roosevelt
(1858-1919) 26th U.S. President

Behold what you stand for and be careful what you fall for.

Ruth Boorstein
Present Day Author

Too many of today's children have straight teeth and crooked morals.

Unknown High School Principal

A conscience cannot prevent sin. It only prevents you from enjoying it.

Harry Hershfield
(1885-1974) Comic Strip Creator, Humorist

216

THE FAMILY

Insightful Observations on
GUILT

Guilt: the gift that keeps on giving.

Erma Bombeck
(1927-1996) Humorist, Author

Guilt is the next best thing to being there.

Ellen Sue Stern
Present Day Relationship
Expert, Writer

Mothers, food, love, and career: the four major guilt groups.

Cathy Guisewite
(1950-) Cartoonist; *Cathy*

Woman, holding a phone, speaking to her husband: It's your mother. She wants to remind you again just how difficult and painful your birth was.

Christopher Weyant
Present Day Cartoonist in
The New Yorker

My mother could make anyone feel guilty—she used to get letters of apology from people she didn't even know.

Joan Rivers
(1933-) Actress, Comedian

When I was a kid, my mother switched religions from Catholic to Episcopalian. Which is what, Catholic Lite? One-third less guilt than regular religion.

Rick Corso
Present Day Comedian,
Actor

Hello, Arthur. This is your mother. Do you remember me?…Someday you'll get married and have children of your own and Honey, when you do, I only pray that they'll make you suffer the way you're making me. That's a Mother's Prayer.

Mike Nichols
(1931-) Director,
Screenwriter

 = IDEALIST   = REALIST   = CYNIC

HAVING BABIES

CHILDHOOD

TEENAGERS

PARENTING

HOME LIFE

RELATIVES

THE FAMILY

Insightful Observations on
SPIRITUALITY & FAMILY

An ounce of mother is worth a pound of clergy.

 Spanish Proverb

We are given children to test us and make us more spiritual.

George Will
(1941-) Political Syndicated Columnist, TV Journalist

When God wants an important thing done in this world or a wrong righted, He goes about it in a very singular way. He doesn't release thunderbolts or stir up earthquakes. God simply has a tiny baby born, perhaps of a very humble home, perhaps of a very humble mother. And God puts the idea or purpose into the mother's heart. And she puts it in the baby's mind, and then—God waits.

Edmond McDonald
20th Century Presbyterian Writer

There's nothing that can help you understand your beliefs more than trying to explain them to an inquisitive child.

Frank A. Clark
Present Day Author

My children have a Higher Power and it's not me.

Carolyn White
20th Century Author

A group of closely related persons living under one roof; it is a convenience, often a necessity, sometimes a pleasure, sometimes the reverse; but who first exalted it as admirable, an almost religious ideal?

Rose Macaulay
(1889-1958) British Writer

Fortunately, my parents were intelligent, enlightened people. They accepted me for what I was: a punishment from God.

 David Steinberg
(1942-) Comedian, Actor

THE FAMILY

Insightful Observations on
KIDS & RELIGION

The family that prays together stays together.

 Proverb

An exasperated mother, whose son was always getting into mischief, finally asked him, "How do you expect to get into Heaven?" The boy thought it over and said, "Well, I'll just run in and out, and in and out, and keep slamming the door until St. Peter says, 'For Heaven's sake, Jimmy, come in or stay out!'"

 Author Unknown

When I was a kid, I used to pray every night for a new bicycle. Then I realized that the Lord, in his wisdom, didn't work that way. So I just stole one and asked him to forgive me.

 Emo Philips
Present Day Comedian

When I was little, my mother heard me playing "church." Apparently, God was in the class and misbehaving, whereupon I told God to "sit down and shut up." Her first thought was to tell me not to talk to God in that way, but then she thought it was better that I had such a close and friendly relationship with the deity.

 Pam Beer
Present Day Author

If a kid asks where rain comes from, I think a cute thing to tell him is God is crying. And if he asks why God is crying, another cute thing to tell him is, "Probably because of something you did."

 Emo Philips
Present Day Comedian

You better pray that will come out of the carpet!

 Anonymous Mother

HAVING BABIES

CHILDHOOD

TEENAGERS

PARENTING

HOME LIFE

RELATIVES

HAVING BABIES

CHILDHOOD

TEENAGERS

PARENTING

HOME LIFE

RELATIVES

THE HOME

Insightful Observations on
BUYING A HOME

No man feels more of a man in the world if he have but a bit of ground that he can call his own. However small it is on the surface, it is four thousand miles deep; and that is a very handsome property.

Charles Dudley Warner
(1829-1900) Editor, Writer

We live in a mobile home. Hey, there are advantages to living in a mobile home. One time, it caught on fire. We met the fire department halfway there.

Ronnie Shakes
Present Day Author, Humorist

LUCY: That house won't be ours for twenty years.
RICKY: Now, honey. Now, now. There's nothing to cry about.
LUCY: Oh no? I just figured out how old I'll be in twenty years!

I Love Lucy
TV Sitcom (1951-1957)

People are living longer than ever before, a phenomenon undoubtedly made necessary by the 30-year mortgage.

Doug Larson
Present Day Cartoonist

The universe is merely a fleeting idea in God's mind—a pretty uncomfortable thought, particularly if you've just made a down payment on a house.

Woody Allen
(1935-) Director, Actor, Writer

THE HOME

Insightful Observations on
THE MEANING OF A HOME

Home is where the heart is.

Pliny The Elder
(23-79) Ancient Author;
Scientist

"Home" is any four walls that enclose the right person.

Helen Rowland
(1876-1958) Novelist,
Playwright

Where we love is home—home that our feet may leave, but not our hearts.

Oliver Wendell Holmes Sr.
(1809-1894) Writer; Physician

I hated my marriage, but I always had a great place to park.

Gerald Nachman
20th Century Columnist,
Author

Marriage isn't that big of a deal anymore; it's so easy to get divorced. You want a commitment? Buy a house. It's funny how the fear of foreclosure has a way of strengthening the male-female bond. Nothing says love like thirty years of debt together.

Tom Pecora
Present Day Comedian

Home is the cornerstone of the American Life. Living in it is a pain in the neck.

Elizabeth Hawes
(1903-1971) Fashion Designer;
Author

House, n. A hollow edifice erected for the habitation of man, rat, mouse, beetle, cockroach, fly, mosquito, flea, bacillus, and microbe.

Ambrose Bierce
(1842-1914) Writer; *The Devil's Dictionary*

INSIGHTFUL OBSERVATIONS TO SHARE

221

THE HOME

Insightful Observations on
HOME ATMOSPHERE

A comfortable house is a great source of happiness. It ranks immediately after health and a good conscience.

Sydney Smith
(1909-1978) Actor

Life is crazy. Now, maybe you knew this all along. But before I had children, I actually held on to the illusion that there was some sense of order to the universe… I am now convinced that we are all living in a Chagall painting —a world where brides and grooms and cows and chickens and angels and sneakers are all mixed up together, sometimes floating in the air, sometimes upside down and everywhere.

Susan Lapinksi
20th Century Author,
Journalist

The Kennedy home was a place of much action and laughter, a lively, brawling mob of children overseen by a mother who knew when to look the other way.

James David Barber
(1930-) Author, Chairman of
Amnesty International

I have always thought that there is no more fruitful source of family discontent than badly cooked dinners and untidy ways.

Isabella Beeton
(1836-1865) Culinary &
Housekeeping Expert, Author

We had a depression fair in the backyard. A major game there was Pin the Blame on the Donkey.

Richard Lewis
(1947-) Comedian, Actor

Having a family is like having a bowling alley installed in your brain.

Martin Mull
(1943-) Actor, Producer,
Writer, Comedian

My parents only had one argument in forty-five years. It lasted forty-three years.

Cathy Ladman
(1955-) Comedian

222

THE HOME

Insightful Observations on
HOME COOKING

I had a bag of Fritos, they were Texas-grilled Fritos. These Fritos had grill marks on them. They reminded me of something: when we used to fire up the barbecue and throw down some Fritos. I can still see my dad with the apron on: "Better flip that Frito, Dad. You know how I like mine."

Mitch Hedberg
(1968-) Actor, Director, Writer

Men like to barbecue. Men will cook if danger is involved.

Rita Rudner
(1956-) Comedian

My cooking was and still is about the worst in America. George is so kind about it.

Barbara Bush
(1925-) Wife of 41st U.S. President George Bush Sr.

The most remarkable thing about my mother is that for thirty years she served the family nothing but leftovers. The original meal has never been found.

Calvin Trillin
(1935-) Author, Humorist

I never see any home cooking. All I get is this fancy stuff.

Prince Phillip
(1921-) Duke of Edinbergh

I come from a home where gravy is a beverage.

Erma Bombeck
(1927-1996) Humorist, Author

My mother's cooking consisted of two choices: take it or leave it.

Buddy Hackett
(1924-2003) Actor, Comedian

 = IDEALIST   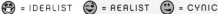 = REALIST   ☺ = CYNIC

223

HAVING BABIES

CHILDHOOD

TEENAGERS

PARENTING

HOME LIFE

RELATIVES

THE HOME

Insightful Observations on
HOME APPEARANCE

If you want a golden rule that will fit everything, this is it: Have nothing in your house that you do not know to be useful or believe to be beautiful.

William Morris
(1834-1896) Founder of the Arts and Crafts Movement

Children are a house's enemy. They don't mean to be—they just can't help it. It's their enthusiasm, their energy, their naturally destructive tendencies.

Delia Ephron
Present Day Writer, Producer

If you're running late, set the table and start cooking an onion. When your husband gets home, he'll think you've been cooking all day.

Author Unknown

If your house is really a mess and a stranger comes to the door, greet him with, "Who could have done this? We have no enemies."

Phyllis Diller
(1917-) Comedian, Actress, Author

Don't cook. Don't clean. No man will ever make love to a woman because she waxed the linoleum—"My God, the floor's immaculate. Lie down, you hot b__tch."

Joan Rivers
(1933-) Actress, Comedian

There is no more somber enemy of good art than the pram (stroller) in the hall.

Cyril Connolly
(1903-1974) British Journalist

Cleaning your house while your kids are still growing is like shoveling the walk before it stops snowing.

Phyllis Diller
(1917-) Comedian, Actress, Author

THE HOME

Insightful Observations on
HOME MAINTENANCE

I am grateful for the lawn that needs mowing, windows that need cleaning, and floors that need waxing because it means I have a home.

 Author Unknown

A perfect summer day is when the sun is shining, the breeze is blowing, the birds are singing, and the lawn mower is broken.

James Dent
20th Century Humorist

One only needs two tools in life: WD-40 to make things go, and duct tape to make them stop.

G.M. Weilacher
20th Century Humorist

I want a house that has got over all its troubles; I don't want to spend the rest of my life bringing up a young and inexperienced house.

Jerome K. Jerome
(1859-1927) Author

The fellow that owns his own home is always just coming out of a hardware store.

Kin Hubbard
(1868-1930) Journalist, Humorist

I always thought a yard was three feet, then I started mowing the lawn.

C.E. Cowman
20th Century Author

Some primal termite knocked on wood
And tasted it, and found it good,
And that is why your Cousin May
Fell through the parlor floor today.

Ogden Nash
(1902-1971) Poet, Humorist

HAVING BABIES

CHILDHOOD

TEENAGERS

PARENTING

HOME LIFE

RELATIVES

HAVING BABIES

CHILDHOOD

TEENAGERS

PARENTING

HOME LIFE

RELATIVES

THE HOME

Insightful Observations on
DOING HOUSEWORK

I hate doing laundry. I don't separate the colors from the whites. I put them together and let them learn from their cultural differences.

Rita Rudner
(1956-) Comedian

Housework is what a woman does that nobody notices unless she hasn't done it.

Evan Esar
(1899-1995) Writer

The darn trouble with cleaning the house is it gets dirty the next day anyway, so skip a week if you have to. The children are the most important thing.

Barbara Bush
(1925-) Wife of 41st U.S.
President George Bush Sr.

Men build bridges and throw railroads across deserts, and yet they contend successfully that the job of sewing on a button is beyond them. Accordingly, they don't have to sew buttons.

Heywood Broun
(1888-1939) Journalist

I do my half. I do half of his half, and the rest doesn't get done.

Arlie Hochschild
20th Century Sociologist,
Author

Housework won't kill you, but why take a chance?

Phyllis Diller
(1917-) Comedian, Actress,
Author

THE HOME

Insightful Observations on
WOMEN & HOUSEWORK

HAVING BABIES

CHILDHOOD

TEENAGERS

PARENTING

HOME LIFE

RELATIVES

Love is the thing that enables a woman to sing while she mops up the floor after her husband has walked across it in his barn boots.

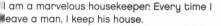

Hoosier Farmer
Indiana Farm Bureau's quarterly magazine

I am a marvelous housekeeper. Every time I leave a man, I keep his house.

Zsa Zsa Gabor
(1917-) Hungarian Actress

My theory on housework is, if the item doesn't multiply, smell, catch on fire or block the refrigerator door, let it be. No one cares. Why should you?

Erma Bombeck
(1927-1996) Humorist, Author

I don't know what liberation can do about it, but even when the man helps, a woman's work is never done.

Beryl Pfizer
20th Century Journalist,
Former "Today Girl"

Nature abhors a vacuum. And so do I.

Anne Gibbons
Present Day Cartoonist,
Humorist

When they come up with a riding vacuum cleaner, then I'll clean the house.

Roseanne Barr
(1952-) Actress, Comedian,
Talk Show Host, Producer

THE HOME

Insightful Observations on
MEN & HOUSEWORK

I got the blues thinking of the future, so I left off and made some marmalade. It's amazing how it cheers one up to shred oranges and scrub the floor.

D.H. Lawrence
(1885-1930) Novelist, Poet, Essayist

Who wears the pants in the house? I do, and I also wash and iron them.

Dennis Thatcher
(1915-2003) Husband of British Prime Minister Margaret Thatcher

The obvious and fair solution to the housework problem is to let men do the housework for, say, the next six thousand years, to even things up. The trouble is that men, over the years, have developed an inflated notion of the importance of everything they do, so that before long they would turn housework into just as much of a charade as business is now. They would hire secretaries and buy computers and fly off to housework conferences in Bermuda, but they'd never clean anything.

Dave Barry
(1947-) Author, Humorist

This is a honeydew day. That is when you get a day off and the wife says, "Honey, do this," and "Honey, do that" around the house.

Jim Lemon
(1928-) Professional Baseball Player

No man who has wrestled with a self-adjusting card table can ever quite be the man he once was.

James Thurber
(1894-1961) American Cartoonist, Author

I have been married to one Marxist and one Fascist, and neither one would take out the garbage.

Lee Grant
(1927-) Actress, Director, Writer

228

Sidebar labels: HAVING BABIES • CHILDHOOD • TEENAGERS • PARENTING • HOME LIFE • RELATIVES

THE HOME

Insightful Observations on KIDS & CHORES

Any kid will run an errand for you if you ask at bedtime.

Red Skelton
(1913-1997) Actor, Composer, Producer

Teenagers who are never required to vacuum are living in one.

Fred G. Gosman
Present Day Author

My kids always perceived the bathroom as a place where you wait it out until all the groceries are unloaded from the car.

Erma Bombeck
(1927-1996) Humorist, Author

There are three ways to get something done: do it yourself, hire someone, or forbid your kids to do it.

Author Unknown

Freud is all nonsense; the secret of neurosis is to be found in the family battle of wills to see who can refuse longest to help with the dishes. The sink is the great symbol of the bloodiness of family life.

Julian Mitchel
(1935-) Author, Screenwriter

Is it possible that my sons-in-law will do toilets? If we raise boys to know that diapers need to be changed and cleaned, there's hope for the next generation.

Anne Roiphe
Present Day Author

 = IDEALIST   = REALIST   😊 = CYNIC

HAVING BABIES

CHILDHOOD

TEENAGERS

PARENTING

HOME LIFE

RELATIVES

THE HOME

Insightful Observations on
TOYS IN THE HOME

You will always be your child's favorite toy.

Vicky Lanksy
Present Day Parenting
Expert, Author

If Barbie is so popular, why do you have to buy her friends?

Steven Wright
(1955-) Actor, Writer,
Comedian

It costs more now to amuse a child than it once did to educate his father.

Vaughan Monroe
(1911-1973) Actor, Writer, TV
Show Host

The site of the true bottomless financial pit is the toy store. It's amazing how much a few pieces of plastic and paper will sell for if the purchasers are parents or grandparents, especially when the manufacturers claim their product improves a child's intellectual or physical development.

**Lawrence Kutner,
Ph.D**
20th Century Psychologist,
Author, Columnist,
Professor

Everyone who ever walked barefoot into his child's room late at night hates LEGOs.

Tony Kornheiser
Present Day Sports
Columnist, Writer, TV Show
Host

Toys are made in heaven, batteries are made in hell.

Tom Robbins
(1936-) Author

New! Divorced Barbie. Barbie with all of Ken's accessories.

Author Unknown

THE HOME

Insightful Observations on BROKEN HOMES

My parents' divorce made me want to make my marriage work.

 Denzel Washington
(1954-) Actor

Yes, single-parent families are different from two-parent families. And urban families are different from rural ones, and families with six kids and a dog are different from one-child, no-pet households. But even if there is only one adult presiding at the dinner table, yours is every bit as much a real family as are the Walton's.

 Marge Kennedy
Present Day Author

Divorces don't wreck children's live. People do.

 Fred Rogers
(1928-2003) Creator & Host of TV show; *Mister Roger's Neighborhood*

According to an article in the USA Today, children from single-parent homes have much better verbal skills than children from two-parent homes. However, children from two-parent homes are far superior at bitterly sarcastic repartee.

 Dennis Miller
(1953-) Actor, Comedian

When I can no longer bear to think of the victims of broken homes, I begin to think of the victims of intact ones.

 Peter De Vries
(1910-1993) Editor, Writer

We would have broken up except for the children. Who were the children? Well, she and I were.

 Mort Sahl
(1927-) Comedian, Actor

HAVING BABIES

CHILDHOOD

TEENAGERS

PARENTING

HOME LIFE

RELATIVES

HAVING BABIES

CHILDHOOD

TEENAGERS

PARENTING

HOME LIFE

RELATIVES

MONEY

Insightful Observations on
BEING BORN RICH

A card carrying member of the lucky sperm club.

George Brightman
Present Day Cigar
Aficionado, Raconteur

Money is better than poverty. If only for financial reasons.

Woody Allen
(1935-) Director, Actor,
Writer

Give me the life of the boy whose mother is nurse, seamstress, washerwoman, cook, teacher, angel, and saint, all in one, and whose father is guide, exemplar, and friend. No servants to come between. These are the boys who are born to the best fortune.

Andrew Carnegie
(1835-1919) American
Industrialist, Philanthropist

Being born rich is like winning the lottery out of the gate, only better, because it often comes with a plan to make more and great baby clothes.

Oscar Herman
(1909-1980) Humorist, Shoe
Salesman

No McTavish
Was ever so lavish.

Ogden Nash
(1902-1971) Poet, Humorist

Some people are born on third base and go through life thinking they hit a triple.

Barry Switzer
(1937-) College &
Professional Football
Coach

Good families are generally worse than any others.

Sir Anthony Hope Hawkins
(1863-1933) British Novelist

MONEY

Insightful Observations on
BEING BORN POOR

I don't care how poor a man is; if he has family, he's rich.

Harry Morgan
as Colonel Potter in
*M*A*S*H* TV Show (1972-1983)

Father talking to son: Do you ever stop to think about the nepotism issues I've spared you?

William Hamilton
Present Day Cartoonist in
The New Yorker

I've never been poor, only broke. Broke is a temporary situation, being poor is a frame of mind.

Mike Todd
(1909-1958) Film Producer

Another good thing about being poor is that, when you are seventy, your children will not have you declared legally insane in order to gain control of your estate.

Woody Allen
(1935-) Director, Actor, Writer

I could now afford all the things I never had as a kid, if I didn't have kids.

Robert Orben
(1927-) Author, Humorist

My family was too poor to have children, so the neighbors had me.

Buddy Hackett
(1924-2003) Actor, Comedian

My family was so poor, we used to go to Kentucky Fried Chicken and lick other peoples' fingers.

Snaps
(1994) a book by James Percelay

HAVING BABIES

CHILDHOOD

TEENAGERS

PARENTING

HOME LIFE

RELATIVES

MONEY

Insightful Observations on
THE VALUE OF MONEY

Youth is the best time to be rich, and the best time to be poor.

 Euripides
(484-407BC) Greek Dramatist

The easiest way for your children to learn about money is for you not to have any.

Katherine Whitehorn
(1928-) British Columnist, Author

I didn't want to be rich, I just wanted to have enough money to get the couch re-upholstered.

Kate Mostel
(1944-1977) Dancer, Wife of Zero Mostel

Trying to give children everything is often worse than to give children nothing.

Marcelene Cox
20th Century Writer, Columnist

It is frequently said that children do not know the value of money. This is only partially true. They do not know the value of your money. Their money, they know the value of.

Judy Markey
(1944-) Author, Radio Talk Show Host

When I was kidnapped, my parents snapped into action. They rented out my room.

Woody Allen
(1935-) Director, Actor, Writer

Son, you're all grown up now. You owe me two hundred and fourteen thousand dollars.

Robert Weber
Present Day Cartoonist in *The New Yorker*

THE GUIDE TO LAUGHING AT FAMILY

MONEY

Insightful Observations on
ALLOWANCE

Young girl says to her father who is sitting in a chair reading a newspaper: I need some short-term economic stimulus.

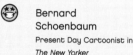 Bernard
Schoenbaum
Present Day Cartoonist in
The New Yorker

The best time to start giving your children money is when they will no longer eat it.

 Barbara Coloroso
Present Day Author, Parent
Educator

When the history of guilt is written, parents who refuse their children money will be right up here in the Top Ten.

Erma Bombeck
(1927-1996) Humorist, Author

It was tough asking thrifty parents for money. You've got to beg fathers: "Dad, can I have a dollar?" "What happened to the dollar I gave you last year?"

Sinbad
(1956-) Comedian, Actor,
Writer

HAVING BABIES

CHILDHOOD

TEENAGERS

PARENTING

HOME LIFE

RELATIVES

 = IDEALIST = REALIST 😊 = CYNIC

MONEY

Insightful Observations on SAVING MONEY

Misers aren't fun to live with, but they make wonderful ancestors.

 David Brenner
(1945-) Comedian

It is not economical to go to bed early to save the candles if the result is twins.

 Chinese Proverb

The trouble with the average family is it has too much month left over at the end of the money.

 Bill Vaughan
(1915-1977) Journalist, Author

Some couples go over their budgets very carefully each month, others just go over them.

 Sally Poplin
Present Day Humorist

My mother had to send me to the movies with my birth certificate, so I wouldn't have to pay the extra fifty cents (the adults had to pay).

 Kareem Abdul-Jabbar
(1947-) Hall of Fame, Professional Basketball Player

Have you any idea how many children it takes to turn off one light in the kitchen? Three. It takes one to say, "What light?" and two more to say, "I didn't turn it on."

 Erma Bombeck
(1927-1996) Humorist, Author

HAVING BABIES

CHILDHOOD

TEENAGERS

PARENTING

HOME LIFE

RELATIVES

FAMILY GATHERINGS

Insightful Observations on
CHILDREN'S PARTIES

Every time a baby's existence…is celebrated, a tiny piece is added to the foundation of that baby's future self-image, self-confidence and social competence.

 Penelope Leach
(1937-) Child Developmental Psychologist, Author

Listen to a random group of Americans attempting to sing "Happy Birthday" and you will note that at any given moment they somehow manage to emit more different notes, total, than there are group members, creating a somber, droning sound such as might be created by severely asthmatic bagpipers, so that the birthday person, rather than feeling happy, winds up weeping into the cake.

Dave Barry
(1947-) Author, Humorist

I had the worst birthday party ever when I was a child, because my parents hired a pony to give rides. These ponies are never in good health, but this one dropped dead. It just wasn't much fun after that. One kid would sit on him and the rest of us would drag him around in a circle.

Rita Rudner
(1956-) Comedian

I have just returned from a children's party. I am one of the survivors. There are not many of us.

 Percy French
(1854-1920) Irish Engineer, Songwriter

The problem with children is that you have to put up with their parents.

 Charles DeLint
(1951-) Canadian Writer, Artist, Musician

HAVING BABIES

CHILDHOOD

TEENAGERS

PARENTING

HOME LIFE

RELATIVES

FAMILY GATHERINGS

Insightful Observations on
MOTHER'S DAY

Mother's Day is the biggest day of the year for long distance phone calls. Makes you wonder why so many people move long distances from Mom, doesn't it?

David Letterman
(1947-) Humorist, Talk Show Host

Unpleasant questions are being raised about Mother's Day. Is this day necessary?... Isn't it bad public policy?... No politician with half his senses, which a majority of politicians have, is likely to vote for its abolition, however. As a class, mothers are tender and loving, but as a voting block they would not hesitate for an instant to pull the seat out from under any Congressman who suggests that Mother is not entitled to a box of chocolates each year in the middle of May.

Russell Baker
(1925-) Columnist, Humorist

Spend at least one Mother's Day with your respective husbands before you decide on marriage. If a man gives his mother a gift certificate for a flu shot, dump him.

Erma Bombeck
(1927-1996) Humorist, Author

A printed card means nothing except that you are too lazy to write to the woman who has done more for you than anyone in the world. And candy! You take a box to Mother—and then eat most of it yourself. A pretty sentiment.

Anna Jarvis
(1864-1907) Founder of Mother's Day; **she squandered Mom's entire estate on a campaign to prevent the Hallmarking of the holiday**

238

FAMILY GATHERINGS

Insightful Observations on FATHER'S DAY

Fatherhood is pretending the present you love most is soap-on-a-rope.

 Bill Cosby
(1937-) Comedian, Actor, Producer

Father's Day is like Mother's Day, except the gift is cheaper

 Gerald F. Lieberman
20th Century Writer

CLIFF HUXTABLE: (Holding a ridiculous tie he got for Father's Day) I am sure, somewhere, there is a suit that goes with this tie. Don't get me the suit!

 Bill Cosby
on *The Cosby Show* (1984-1992) created by Bill Cosby

Last Father's Day, my son gave me something I've always wanted—the keys to my car.

 Author Unknown

One of the disadvantages of having children is that they eventually get old enough to give you presents they make at school.

 Robert Byrne
(1930-) Author, Humorist

I can always count on getting one thing for Father's Day—all the bills from Mother's Day.

 Milton Berle
(1908-2002) Comedian, Actor, TV Personality

HAVING BABIES

CHILDHOOD

TEENAGERS

PARENTING

HOME LIFE

RELATIVES

HAVING BABIES

CHILDHOOD

TEENAGERS

PARENTING

HOME LIFE

RELATIVES

FAMILY GATHERINGS

Insightful Observations on
HALLOWEEN

The first time you hear the concept of Halloween when you're a kid, your brain can't even process the idea. You're like, "What is this? What did you say? Someone's giving out candy? Who's giving out candy? Everyone we know is just giving out candy? I gotta be a part of this!"

Jerry Seinfeld
(1954-) Comedian, Actor, Producer

Halloween was confusing. All my life my parents said, "Never take candy from strangers." And then they dressed me up and said, "Go beg for it." I didn't know what to do. I'd knock on people's doors and go, "Trick or treat. No thank you."

Rita Rudner
(1956-) Comedian

I remember my first Halloween wanting very badly to be a devil. I remember making a very big deal about it and my mother finally making me a devil costume for me by hand. In subsequent years I became more sophisticated image-protection-wise and chose costumes that were not so candid.

Jerry Seinfeld
(1954-) Comedian, Actor, Producer

I learned something the other day. I learned that Jehovah's Witnesses do not celebrate Halloween. I guess they don't like strangers going up to their door and annoying them.

Bruce Clark
Present Day Comedian

240

FAMILY GATHERINGS

Insightful Observations on
THANKSGIVING

What we're really talking about is a wonderful day set aside on the fourth Thursday of November when no one diets. I mean, why else would they call it Thanksgiving?

Erma Bombeck
(1927-1996) Humorist, Author

This Thanksgiving is gonna be a special one. My mom says I don't have to sit at the card table.

Jim Samuels
(1948-1990) Comedian

We are having the usual thing for our Thanksgiving dinner: relatives.

Author Unknown

The latest thing in L.A. is adopting a turkey. I adopted one. I also adopted some cranberry sauce, some mashed potatoes…

Jay Leno
(1950-) Comedian, Talk Show Host

I celebrated Thanksgiving in the traditional way. I invited everyone in my neighborhood to my house, we had an enormous feast. And then I killed them and took their land.

Jon Stewart
(1962-) Actor, Writer, TV talk Show Host

Thanksgiving is an emotional holiday. People travel thousands of miles to be with people they only see once a year. And then discover once a year is way too often.

Johnny Carson
(1925-) Comedian, Talk Show Host

Thanksgiving, or as Fox calls it, When Relatives Attack.

Jay Leno
(1950-) Comedian, Talk Show Host

 = IDEALIST  = REALIST   = CYNIC

FAMILY GATHERINGS

Insightful Observations on
FAMILY HOLIDAYS

Blessed is the season which engages the whole world in a conspiracy of love!

 Hamilton Wright Mabie
(1845-1916) Author, Editor, Critic

Be sure you count the Easter eggs before you hide them.

 Author Unkown

No self-respecting mother would run out of intimidations on the eve of a major holiday.

 Erma Bombeck
(1927-1996) Humorist, Author

My family is Jewish, so on holidays we eat these big, heavy, starchy meals. In honor of Jewish cooking, our next holiday will be called the Festival of Tums.

 Fran Chernowsky
Present Day Comedian

Santa Claus has the right idea. Visit people once a year.

 Victor Borge
(1909-2000) Comedian;
"Clown Prince of Denmark"

HAVING BABIES

CHILDHOOD

TEENAGERS

PARENTING

HOME LIFE

RELATIVES

FAMILY GATHERINGS

Insightful Observations on
CHRISTMAS TIME

Never worry about the size of your Christmas tree. In the eyes of children, they are all 30 feet tall.

 Larry Wilde
20th Century Motivational Speaker; Humorist, Author; *The Merry Book of Christmas*

There has been only one Christmas—the rest are anniversaries.

 W.J. Cameron
20th Century Editor of the *Dearborn Independent*

Probably the worst thing about being Jewish during Christmas time is shopping in stores, because the lines are so long. They should have a Jewish express line: "Look, I'm a Jew, it's not a gift. It's just paper towels."

Sue Kolinsky
Modern Day Comedian

If you want to restore your faith in humanity, think about Christmas. If you want to destroy it again, think about Christmas shopping. But the gifts aren't the important thing about the holidays. The important thing is having your family around resenting you.

 Reno Goodale
Present Day Comedian

Christmas is a time when you get homesick—even when you're home.

Carol Nelson
Present Day Comedian

FAMILY GATHERINGS

Insightful Observations on
KIDS & CHRISTMAS

Christmas, children, is not a date. It is a state of mind.

Mary Ellen Chase
(1887-1973) Christian Writer,
Educator

Happy, happy Christmas, that can win us back to the delusions of our childish days; that can recall to the old man the pleasures of his youth; that can transport the sailor and the traveler, thousands of miles away, back to his own fire-side and his quiet home!

Charles Dickens
(1812-1870) British Author

My six-year-old nephew couldn't understand why I bought toys to give to charity for poor kids. Couldn't those kids wait for Santa's free toys to come Christmas Day? I broke down and told him the truth. That Santa Claus is a Republican.

Brenda Pontiff
Present Day Comedian,
Actor

Christmas always sucked when I was a kid because I believed in Santa Claus. Unfortunately, so did my parents. So I never got anything.

Charlie Viracola
Present Day Comedian

FAMILY GATHERINGS

Insightful Observations on
FAMILY OUTINGS

There is no such thing as fun for the whole family.

 Jerry Seinfeld
(1954-) Comedian, Actor, Producer

At the end of your life you will never regret not having passed one more test, not winning one more verdict, or not closing one more deal. You will regret time not spent with a husband, a friend, a child or a parent.

 Author Unknown

I was overjoyed when the family could join me in New York for a couple of months in the summer, and I wanted to make sure the children didn't get sore at me for jerking them out of Oklahoma right during vacation time—which, in spite of the heat, is naturally the best time of the year to them. So I told my wife, "Even if I'm at work, keep the kids amused." That accounts for my wife taking them to New York's famous Natural History Museum, with all its stuffed animal exhibits—mounted zebras, lions, hippopotamuses, elephants, mountain goats, and so on. That night I asked Linda what she had seen. When she proved hesitant, I said, "Come on, you don't have to make it a long story. Just name it. What did you see?" Her eyes twinkled. "I saw a dead circus."

Cal Tinney
(1908-) Comedian; famous for saying,"stop me if you heard this one"

My family is really boring. They have a coffee table book called Pictures We Took Just to Use Up the Rest of the Film.

 Penelope Lombard
Present Day Comedian, Actor

My parents used to take me to the pet department and tell me it was a zoo.

 Billy Connolly
(1942-) Actor, Writer

INSIGHTFUL OBSERVATIONS TO SHARE

HAVING BABIES

CHILDHOOD

TEENAGERS

PARENTING

HOME LIFE

RELATIVES

FAMILY GATHERINGS

Insightful Observations on
FAMILY VACATIONS

Babies don't need vacations, but I still see them at the beach.

Steven Wright
(1955-) Actor, Writer, Comedian

In America there are two classes of travel—first class, and with children.

Robert Benchley
(1889-1945) Writer, Humorist, Actor

A vacation frequently means that the family goes away for a rest, accompanied by a mother who sees that the others get it.

Marcelene Cox
20th Century Writer, Columnist

...In times of great stress, such as the four-day vacation, the thin veneer of family life wears off almost at once, and we are revealed in our true personalities.

Shirley Jackson
(1919-1965) Author

Whenever we take trips, we have to enlist the help of thirteen sherpas, a chauffeur, two maids and a nanny—and that's only for the baby's luggage.

Ginger Hinchman
Present Day Author

A family vacation is one where you arrive with five bags, four kids and seven I-thought-you-packed-its.

Ivern Ball
20th Century Columnist

When my husband and I go on trips I get two jobs in the car: I get to read the map and I get to ask for directions when we get lost.

Rita Rudner
(1956-) Comedian

246

FAMILY GATHERINGS

Insightful Observations on FAMILY MEALS

A smiling face is half the meal.

 Latvian Proverb

Everybody has casserole memories.

 Julia Reed
Present Day *New York Times Magazine* Columnist

After a good dinner one can forgive anybody, even one's own relatives.

 Oscar Wilde
(1854-1900) Poet, Playwright, Novelist

When my mother had dinner for eight, she'd make enough for 16 and only serve half.

 Gracie Allen
(1902-1964) Comedian, Radio & TV Personality

It's a mistake to think you can solve any major problem with just potatoes.

 Douglas Adams
(1952-2001) English Author

If it weren't for Philo T. Farnsworth, the inventor of the television, we'd be eating frozen radio dinners.

 Johnny Carson
(1925-) Comedian, Talk Show Host

Family dinners are more often than not an ordeal of nervous indigestion, preceded by hidden resentment and ennui and accompanied by psychosomatic jitters.

 M. F. K. Fisher
(1908-1978) Author

 = IDEALIST   = REALIST   = CYNIC

FAMILY GATHERINGS

Insightful Observations on
DINNING OUT

The age of your children is a key factor in how quickly you are served in a restaurant. We once had a waiter in Canada who said, "Could I get you your check?" and we answered, "How about the menu first?"

Erma Bombeck
(1927-1996) Humorist, Author

The other night I ate at a real nice family restaurant. Every table had an argument going.

George Carlin
(1938-) Comedian, Actor, Writer

Children never want to eat in restaurants. What they want is to play under the table until the entrees arrive, then go to the bathroom.

Dave Barry
(1947-) Author, Humorist

Ask your child what he wants for dinner only if he's buying.

Fran Lebowitz
(1950-) Writer, Humorist

FAMILY GATHERINGS

Insightful Observations on
FAMILY SHOPPING

HAVING BABIES

CHILDHOOD

TEENAGERS

PARENTING

HOME LIFE

RELATIVES

LOIS: Oh, come on, Malcolm. If we only looked at stuff we could afford, all we would ever see is crap.

Jane Kaczmarek
to Frankie Muniz in *Malcolm in the Middle* TV Sitcom

Don't go grocery shopping when you are hungry.

Joyce Isaacs
(1937-) Present Day Mom

CLIFF HUXTABLE: No boy should have a $95 shirt unless he is onstage with his four brothers!

Bill Cosby
in *The Cosby Show* (1984-1992)

Supermarkets are like giant booby traps for males—which is why if you send a man out to buy eggs, sugar, and bread you should not be surprised if he returns home with a case of wine, a pair of jeans, and a tree.

Author Unknown

I was doing the family grocery shopping accompanied by two children, an event I hope to see included in the Olympics in the near future.

Anna Quindlen
(1953-) Novelist, Social Critic, Columnist

One quarter of what you buy will turn out to be mistakes.

Delia Ephron
Present Day Writer, Producer

WELLNESS THROUGH LAUGHTER

FAMILY GATHERINGS

Insightful Observations on
CAR POOLING

Other mothers help me with chauffeuring the kids around, and I do the same for them. I believe that in order to do all we need to, we need help, and I've found that others are willing to form a network with you.

Maria Shriver
(1955-) Television Journalist

BERNIE MAC: Okay, first rule of this carpool. No breaking wind in my car. The only gas that Bernie Mac wants to be smelling is unleaded.

Bernie Mac
on *The Bernie Mac Show* TV Sitcom

Onion rings in the car cushions do not improve with time.

Erma Bombeck
(1927-1996) Columnist, Author

You know you've spent too much time carpooling your kids when fast-food, drive-through servers recognize your voice.

Linda Fiterman
Present Day Parenting Expert, Author

Safety was not a big thing when I was growing up. A seat belt was something that got in the way: "Ma, the seat belt is digging into my back." "Stuff it down into the seat. And roll those windows up, you're letting the smoke out."

Margaret Smith
20th Century Comedian

A suburban mother's role is to deliver children obstetrically once, and by car forever after.

Peter De Vries
(1910-1993) Editor, Writer

My hockey mom could beat up your soccer mom.

Author Unknown

250

FAMILY GATHERINGS

Insightful Observations on
SPORTS

HAVING BABIES

CHILDHOOD

TEENAGERS

PARENTING

HOME LIFE

RELATIVES

I'm convinced that every boy, in his heart, would rather steal second base than an automobile.

Justice Tom C. Clark
(1899-1977) U.S. Supreme Court Justice

Who, in their infinite wisdom, decreed that Little League uniforms be white? Certainly not a mother.

Erma Bombeck
(1927-1996) Columnist, Author

The one nice thing about sports is that they prove men do have emotions and are not afraid to show them.

Jane O'Reilly
Present Day Feminist, Humorist, Author

I do not participate in any sport with ambulances at the bottom of a hill.

Erma Bombeck
(1927-1996) Humorist, Author

If it weren't for baseball, many kids wouldn't know what a millionaire looked like.

Phyllis Diller
(1917-) Comedian, Actress, Author

For the parent of a Little Leaguer, a baseball game is simply a nervous breakdown divided into innings.

Earl Wilson
(1907-1987) Columnist

Some parents got into a brawl at their kids' soccer match in New Jersey. They said they were just teaching their children European soccer.

Craig Kilborn
(1962-) Actor, TV Talk Show Host

INSIGHTFUL OBSERVATIONS TO SHARE

Step Six:

RELA

TIVES

Grandparents

Extended Family

Pets

GRANDPARENTS

Insightful Observations on
BEING A GRANDPARENT

A grandparent is old on the outside but young on the inside.

 Author Unknown

Becoming a grandparent is a second chance. For you have a chance to put use to all the things you learned the first time around and may have made mistakes on. It's all love and no discipline. There's no thorn in this rose.

 Dr. Joyce Brothers
(1928-) Psychologist, TV Personality

All elders should have at least one youngster to be "crazy about" and visa versa. Grandparenting supplies the role model for a healthy and fulfilling old age. And grandchildren want grandparents.

 Arthur Kornhaber, M.D.
20th Century Child & Family Psychiatrist

Grandparents range from infantile to mature, just like everybody else.

 Jean Marzollo
Present Day Children's Poet, Author, Illustrator

It is a shock to realize that the very children you yelled at to clean their rooms such a short time ago are now going to be in charge of your grandchildren.

 Susan M. Kettmen
Present Day Author;*The 12 Rules of Grandparenting*

GRANDPARENTS

Insightful Observations on
GRANDPARENT'S ROLE

The simplest toy, one which even the youngest child can operate, is called a grandparent.

 Sam Levenson
(1911-1980) Humorist, Author

Nobody can do for little children what grandparents do. Grandparents sort of sprinkle stardust over the lives of little children.

 Alex Haley
(1921-1992) Author, Biographer

If you see a book, a rocking chair and a grandchild in the same room, don't pass up a chance to read aloud. Instill in your grandchildren a love of reading. It is one of the greatest gifts you can give.

 Barbara Bush
(1925-) Wife of 41st U.S. President George Bush Sr.

Grandparents who want to be truly helpful will do well to keep their mouths shut and their opinions to themselves until these are requested. At that point, if their ideas can be discussed—not as formed opinions but as suggestions to be taken or disregarded—they can be helpful.

 T. Berry Brazelton
(1918-) Baby Doctor, Columnist, Author

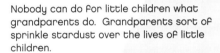 = IDEALIST   = REALIST   = CYNIC

GRANDPARENTS

Insightful Observations on
THE JOY OF GRANDPARENTS

My wife and I often summoned the grandparents of our first baby and cried, "Look, poopoo!"

Bill Cosby
(1937-) Comedian, Actor, Producer

Few things are more delightful than grandchildren fighting over your lap.

Doug Larson
Present Day Cartoonist

Grandchildren are God's way of compensating us for growing old.

Mary H. Waldrip
20th Century Author

They say genes skip generations. Maybe that's why grandparents find their grandchildren so likeable.

Joan McIntosh
Present Day Author

Our grandchildren accept us for ourselves, without rebuke or effort to change us, as no one in our entire lives has ever done, not our parents, siblings, spouses, friends—and hardly ever our own grown children.

Ruth Goode
20th Century Writer

No cowboy was ever faster on the draw than a grandparent pulling a baby picture out of a wallet.

Author Unknown

Getting your grandma a cell phone that sends e-mails and takes pictures is a great way to confuse her three times with one gift.

Craig Kilborn
(1962-) Actor, TV Talk Show Host

256

GRANDPARENTS

Insightful Observations on
CYNICAL GRANDPARENTS

The denunciation of the young is a necessary part of the hygiene of older people, and greatly assists in the circulation of the blood.

Logan Pearsall Smith
(1865-1946) Writer

My grandfather used to make home movies and edit out the joy.

Richard Lewis
(1947-) Actor, Comedian

When I was little, my grandfather one Christmas gave me a box of broken glass. He gave my brother a box of Band-Aids, and said, "You two share."

Steven Wright
(1955-) Actor, Writer, Comedian

When I was little, my grandfather used to make me stand in a closet for five minutes without moving. He said it was elevator practice.

Steven Wright
(1955-) Actor, Writer, Comedian

My grandfather and the talks. The "We Didn't Have Anything in the Old Days" talk. "What happiness? We didn't have happiness in the old days. We were miserable, and we liked it."

Billy Crystal
(1947-) Actor, Comedian

HAVING BABIES

CHILDHOOD

TEENAGERS

PARENTING

HOME LIFE

RELATIVES

GRANDPARENTS

Insightful Observations on
THE GRANDCHILD CONNECTION

I love their home. Everything smelled older, warm but safe; the food aroma had baked itself into the furniture.

Susan Strasburg
(1938-1999) Actor

If I really begged her, Nanny would take her teeth out and smile at me. I never saw anything so funny in my life.

Carol Burnett
(1933-) Actress, Comedian, Singer, Director, Producer, Writer

It's one of nature's way that we often feel closer to distant generations than to the generation immediately preceding us.

Igor Stravinsky
(1882-1971) Composer

Two young boys were spending the night at their grandparents. At bedtime, the two boys kneeled down beside their beds to say their prayers. Suddenly, the youngest boy began praying at the top of his lungs, "I PRAY FOR A NEW BICYCLE. I PRAY FOR A NEW NINTENDO. I PRAY FOR A NEW VCR..." His older brother leaned over, nudged his younger brother, and said, "Why are you shouting your prayers? God isn't deaf." The little brother replied, "No, but Grandma is!"

Author Unknown

Being grandparents sufficiently removes us from the responsibilities so that we can be friends.

Allan Frome
20th Century Writer

The reason grandparents and grandchildren get along so well is that they have a common enemy.

Sam Levenson
(1911-1980) Humorist, Author

GRANDPARENTS

Insightful Observations on
BEING A GRANDFATHER

Every generation revolts against its fathers and makes friends with its grandfathers.

 Lewis Mumford
(1895-1990) Social Philosopher

A baby has a way of making a man out of his father and a boy out of his grandfather

 Angie Papadakis
Present Day Humorist

My granddad used to say, "If everybody liked the same thing, they'd all be after your grandma."

 Gary Muledeer
Present Day Comedian, Actor, TV Personality

My grandfather was in this Russian, this Yiddish circus. He was a Jewish juggler. He used to worry about six things at once.

 Richard Lewis
(1947-) Actor, Comedian

My grandfather had a special rocking chair built that would lean forward rather than backward, so that he could fake interest in any conversation.

 Steven Wright
(1955-) Actor, Writer, Comedian

Grandchildren don't make a man feel old; it's the knowledge that he's married to a grandmother.

G. Norman Collie
19th Century Political & Social Activist

GRANDPARENTS

Insightful Observations on
BEING A GRANDMOTHER

When a child is born, so are grandmothers.

Judith Levy
20th Century Author

Author Unknown

Grandmothers are the people who take delight in hearing babies breathing into the telephone.

If becoming a grandmother was only a matter of choice, I should advise every one of you straight away to become one. There is no fun for old people like it!

Hannah Whithall Smith
(1832-1911) Christian Writer

It's such a grand thing to be a mother of a mother—that's why the world calls her grandmother.

Author Unknown

If your baby is "beautiful and perfect, never cries or fusses, sleeps on schedule and burps on demand, an angel all the time," you're the grandma.

Theresa Bloomingdale
(1930-) Author

A mother becomes a true grandmother the day she stops noticing the terrible things her children do because she is so enchanted with the wonderful things her grandchildren do.

Lois Wyse
Present Day Author;
Columnist; *Funny, You Don't Look Like A Grandmother*

Just about the time a woman thinks her work is done, she becomes a grandmother.

Edward H. Dreschnack
20th Century Author

THE GUIDE TO LAUGHING AT FAMILY

GRANDPARENTS

Insightful Observations on
GRANDMOTHER'S ROLE

Grandmas are moms with lots of frosting.

 Author Unknown

Grandmothers are to life what the Ph.D. is to education. There is nothing you can feel, taste, expect, predict, or want that the grandmothers in your family do not know about in detail.

 Lois Wyse
Present Day Author;
Columnist; *Funny, You Don't Look Like a Grandmother*

A grandmother is a person who has way too much wisdom to let that stop her from making a fool of herself over her grandchildren.

 Author Unknown

A grandmother pretends she doesn't know who you are on Halloween.

 Erma Bombeck
(1927-1996) Humorist, Author

If nothing is going well, call your grandmother.

 Italian Proverb

A grandmother is a babysitter who watches the kids instead of the television.

 Author Unknown

A Jewish grandmother is watching her grandchild playing on the beach when a huge wave comes and takes him out to sea. She pleads, "Please God, save my only grandson. I beg of you, bring him back." And a big wave comes and washes the boy back onto the beach, good as new. She looks up to heaven and says, "He had a hat!"

 Myron Cohen
(1902-1986) Actor, Comedian

 = IDEALIST   = REALIST   = CYNIC

EXTENDED FAMILY

Insightful Observations on
AUNTS, UNCLES & COUSINS

I'm Charlie's aunt from Brazil—Where the nuts come from.

Brandon Thomas
(1856-1914) British Actor;
Dramatist

Every baby resembles the relative who has the most money.

Luke McLuke
(James Syme Hastings)
20th Century Humorist

I've got cousins galore. Mexicans just spread all their seeds. And the women just pop them out.

Christina Aguilera
(1980-) Pop Singer;
Songwriter

Older Jewish relatives can get away with murder. If they forget the name of something, they can make up a word that sounds like Yiddish. "Darling, pass me the...huucch. No, that's the smeklinbach."

Billy Crystal
(1947-) Actor; Comedian

I've got stepcousins. Think about it—stepcousins—as if cousins aren't worthless enough as it is. Stepcousins—I don't know what to do with these people. I'm not blood-related to them; the only thing I can think of is it's okay to have sex with them.

Judd Apatow
(1968-) Writer; Actor

I have nephews...I remember the first time they stayed with us. My sister-in-law, she calls me—it was after midnight—and she's like, "Did you have a hard time getting the boys to sleep?" I'm like, "Sleep? Girl, we're sitting up drinking liquor playing Nintendo."

Wanda Sykes
(1964-) Comedian, Actress,
Writer

EXTENDED FAMILY

Insightful Observations on
TIME WITH RELATIVES

The nice thing about having relatives' kids around is that they go home.

 Cliff Richard
(1940-) British Pop Singer

Company just drove up, put more water in the soup!

 Mary Alice Magnie
(1929-) Mother

Be tolerant of the human race. Your whole family belongs to it—and some of your spouse's family does too.

 Author Unknown

I'm going home next week. It's a kind of emergency—my parents are coming here.

 Rita Rudner
(1956-) Comedian

My parents have been visiting me for a few days. I just dropped them off at the airport. They leave tomorrow.

 Margaret Smith
20th Century Comedian

Distant relatives are the best kind and the further away, the better.

 Kin Hubbard
(1868-1930) Journalist, Humorist

It wouldn't hurt to be nice would it? "That depends on your threshold of pain."

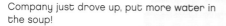 **George S. Kaufman**
(1889-1961) Writer; at age 4, on being told his aunt was coming to visit.

EXTENDED FAMILY

Insightful Observations on
AVOIDING RELATIVES

Many a family tree needs trimming.

 Kin Hubbard
(1868-1930) Journalist, Humorist

It is a melancholy truth that even great men have their poor relations.

 Charles Dickens
(1812-1870) British Novelist

DEBRA BARONE: We got to find a way to get away from your parents.
RAY BARONE: I got the perfect solution—the witness protection program.
DEBRA BARONE: Ray, I'm serious.
RAY BARONE: So am I. Let see them try to find Steve and Phyllis Rosenberg in Tucson, Arizona.

George Burns
(1896-1996) Comedian, Actor

A lot of people would rather tour the sewers than visit their cousins.

 Jane Howard
(1935-1996) Journalist, Writer

Happiness is having a large, loving, caring, close-knit family in another city.

 George Burns
(1896-1996) Comedian, Actor

When my husband and I first got married, our policy on visits to the other's family was 'share the pain'. That soon gave way to our current policy: 'save yourself'.

 Beth Lapides
Present Day Comedian, Actress, Writer

Woman talking on phone: I'm sorry, Mother, we don't respond to telephone solicitations.

 David Sipress
Present Day Cartoonist in *The New Yorker*

THE GUIDE TO LAUGHING AT FAMILY

EXTENDED FAMILY

Insightful Observations on
IN-LAW PROBLEMS

One of the greatest mysteries is how a boy who wasn't good enough to marry your daughter can be the father of the smartest grandchild in the world.

 Jewish Proverb

No mother-in-law ever remembers that she was once a daughter-in-law.

 Author Unknown

My brother-in-law is always there for me when he needs a favor.

 David Corrado
Present Day Humorist

A mother-in-law and a daughter-in-law in one house are like two cats in a bag.

 Yiddish Proverb

All men are brothers, but, thank God, they aren't all brothers-in-law.

 Anthony Powell
(1905-2000) British Novelist

Behind every successful man stands a surprised mother-in law.

 Hurbert Humphrey
(1911-1978) U.S. Vice President, Senator

HAVING BABIES

CHILDHOOD

TEENAGERS

PARENTING

HOME LIFE

RELATIVES

EXTENDED FAMILY

Insightful Observations on
MOTHER-IN-LAW PROBLEMS

What a marvelous place to drop one's mother-in-law!

Marshal Foch
(1851-1929) French Soldier;
remark on being shown the Grand Canyon

If I only had six months to live, I'd move in with my mother-in-law. Because that would be the longest six months of my life.

Oscar Herman
(1909-1980) Humorist, Shoe Salesman

Mechanic talking to car owner: We located the hissing noise, Mr. Watkins. Your wife's mother is in the back seat.

George Booth
Present Day Cartoonist in *The New Yorker*

Never rely on the glory of the morning or the smiles of your mother-in-law.

Japanese Proverb

I haven't spoken to my mother-in-law for eighteen months—I don't like to interrupt her

Kenn Dodd
(1927-) Comedian

.

The mother-in-law thinks I'm effeminate; not that I mind because, beside her, I am.

Les Dawson
(1934-) British Comedian, Writer

Two mothers-in-law.

John, Lord Russell
(1792-1878) British Statesman; **his answer when asked what he would consider a proper punishment for bigamy**

THE GUIDE TO LAUGHING AT FAMILY

PETS

Insightful Observations on
PET'S ROLE

We've begun to long for the pitter-patter of little feet—we bought a dog. Well, it's cheaper, and you get more feet.

Rita Rudner
(1956-) Comedian

It's funny how dogs and cats know the inside of folks better than other folks do, isn't it?

Eleanor H. Porter
(1868-1920) Author

Dogs travel hundreds of miles during their lifetime responding to such commands as "come" and "fetch." Cats approach people only when there is a reason and not always even that.

Stephen Baker
Present Day Author

I have fish for pets. That's what I have. Goldfish. It was originally for the stress thing. They say if you watch fish, it helps you relax, to fall asleep. Which explains why I always doze off when I'm snorkeling.

Ellen Degeneres
(1958-) Actress, Comedian, Talk Show Host

No animal should ever jump up on the dining-room furniture unless absolutely certain that he can hold his own in the conversation.

Fran Lebowitz
(1950-) Writer, Humorist

In order to keep a true perspective of one's importance, everyone should have a dog that will worship him and a cat that will ignore him.

Dereke Rita
Present Day Humorist

 = IDEALIST  = REALIST 😊 = CYNIC

HAVING BABIES

CHILDHOOD

TEENAGERS

PARENTING

HOME LIFE

RELATIVES

PETS

Insightful Observations on LOVING PETS

Dogs are the most amazing creatures; they give unconditional love. For me they are the role model for being alive.

 Gilda Radner
(1946-1989) Actor, Writer

Daddy wouldn't buy me a bow-wow, bow-wow.
I've got a little cat
And I'm very fond of that.

 Joseph Tabrar
(1857-1931) Songwriter

No amount of time can erase the memory of a good cat, and no amount of masking tape can ever totally remove his fur from your couch.

 Leo Dworken
Present Day Humorist

My brother had a hamster. He took it to see the vet; that's like bringing a disposable lighter for repair.

 Wayne Cotter
Present Day Comedian

I've always had pets. I know I should have a child someday, but I wonder, could I love something that doesn't crap in a box?

 Sheila Wenz
Present Day Comedian

The trouble with loving is that pets don't last long enough and people last too long.

 Author Unknown

PETS

Insightful Observations on
DOG RELATIONSHIPS

My goal in life is to be as good of a person my dog already thinks I am.

 Author Unknown

There is no psychiatrist in the world like a puppy licking your face.

 Bern Williams
Present Day Author

My dog and I were working on a new product: It's a combination toilet bowl cleaner and dog breath freshener.

 Robert A. Alper
Present Day Comedian,
Jewish Rabbi

The great pleasure of a dog is that you may make a fool of yourself with him and not only will he not scold you, he will make a fool of himself too.

 Samuel Butler
(1835-1902) British Satirist

Once you have kids, your dog becomes a dog again.

 Bruce Springsteen
(1949-) Singer, Songwriter

They never talk about themselves but listen to you while you talk about yourself, and keep up an appearance of being interested in the conversation.

 Jerome K. Jerome
(1859-1927) Author

Every boy who has a dog should also have a mother, so the dog can be fed regularly.

 Author Unknown

HAVING BABIES

CHILDHOOD

TEENAGERS

PARENTING

HOME LIFE

RELATIVES

PETS

Insightful Observations on
DOG'S LOVE

A dog is the only thing on earth that loves you more than he loves himself.

 Josh Billings
(1818-1885) Humorist

I'm not particularly pre-occupied with the husband/baby thing. Besides I have a dog.

Calista Flockhart
(1964-) Actress

I talk to him when I'm lonesome like; and I'm sure he understands. When he looks at me so attentively, and gently licks my hands; then he rubs his nose on my tailored clothes, but I never say naught thereat. For the good Lord knows I can buy more clothes, but never a friend like that.

W. Dayton Wedgefarth
19th Century Poet

I like dogs. I do. But they're not that bright, really. Let's examine the dog mind. Every time you come home, he thinks it's amazing. He can't believe that you've accomplished this again. You walk in the door. The joy of it almost kills him. "He's back again. It's that guy! It's that guy!"

Jerry Seinfeld
(1954-) Comedian, Actor, Producer

VICKI LARSON: I don't understand why everyone says dogs are man's best friend. Do you really want a best friend who licks his butt before he kisses you?

Gail Edwards
in *Full House* TV Sitcom
(1987-1995)

If dogs could talk, perhaps we would find it as hard to get along with them as we do with people.

 Josef Capek
(1887-1945) Czech Cartoonist

THE GUIDE TO LAUGHING AT FAMILY

PETS

Insightful Observations on
RELATING TO DOGS

You can say any foolish thing to a dog, and the dog will give you a look that says, "You're right! I never would've thought of that!"

 Dave Barry
(1947-) Author, Humorist

Dogs act exactly the way we would act if we had no shame.

Cynthia Heimel
Present Day Writer, Humorist

Dogs laugh, but they laugh with their tails.

Max Eastman
(1883-1969) Author;
Enjoyment of Laughter

If you get to thinkin' you're a person of some influence, try orderin' somebody else's dog around.

Cowboy Wisdom

If you think dogs can't count, try putting three dog biscuits in your pocket and then giving Fido only two of them.

Phil Pastoret
20th Century Journalist

They say the dog is man's best friend. I don't believe that. How many of your friends have you neutered?

Larry Reeb
Present Day Comedian

PETS

Insightful Observations on
THINGS DOGS THINK

Did you ever notice when you blow in a dog's face he gets mad at you? But when you take him in a car he sticks his head out the window.

Steve Bluestone
20th Century Actor, Writer, Humorist

The other day I saw two dogs walk over to a parking meter. One of them says to the other, "How do you like that. Pay toilets."

Dave Starr
20th Century Comedian, Actor

From the dog's point of view, his master is an elongated and abnormally cunning dog.

Mabel Louise Robinson
(1874-1962) Author

I wonder what goes through his mind when he sees us peeing in his water bowl.

Penny Ward Moser
20th Century American Writer

SNOOPY: Yesterday I was a dog. Today I'm a dog. Tomorrow I'll probably still be a dog. Sigh! There's so little hope for advancement.

Charles Schulz
(1922-2000) Cartoonist;
Peanuts

A door is what a dog is perpetually on the wrong side of.

Ogden Nash
(1902-1971) Poet, Humorist

I wonder if other dogs think poodles are members of a weird religious cult.

Rita Rudner
(1956-) Comedian

THE GUIDE TO LAUGHING AT FAMILY

PETS

Insightful Observations on
CAT RELATIONSHIPS

It is impossible to keep a straight face in the presence of one or more kittens.

 Cynthia E. Varnado
Present Day Author

There is something about the presence of a cat that seems to take the bite out of being alone.

 Louis J. Camuti
(1893-1981) Cat Doctor

The cat could very well be man's best friend but would never stoop to admitting it.

 Doug Larson
Present Day Cartoonist

Dogs come when they're called; cats take a message and get back to you later.

 Mary Bly
20th Century Educator, Writer

I had been told that the training procedure with cats was difficult. It's not. Mine had me trained in two days.

 Bill Dana
(1924-) Comedian, Writer, Producer

It's really the cat's house—we just pay the mortgage.

 Author Unknown

 = IDEALIST    = REALIST   = CYNIC

PETS

Insightful Observations on
RELATING TO CATS

Who among us hasn't envied a cat's ability to ignore the cares of daily life and to relax completely?

Karen Brademeyer
Present Day Columnist; *Cat Fancy Magazine*

A cat is a puzzle for which there is no solution.

Hazel Nicholson
Present Day Author

Macavity, Macavity, there's no one like Macavity,
There never was a Cat of such deceitfulness and suavity.
He always has an alibi, and one or two to spare:
At whatever time the deed took place—
MACAVITY WASN'T THERE!

T.S. Eliot
(1888-1965) U.S. Poet, Dramatist, Author

The problem with cats is that they get the exact same look on their face whether they see a moth or an axe-murderer.

Paula Poundstone
(1959-) Comedian, Writer, Actress

I found out why cats drink out of the toilet. My mother told me it's because the water is cold in there. And I'm like, how did my mother know that?

Wendy Liebman
(1961-) Comedian

Cats are intended to teach us that not everything in nature has a purpose.

Garrison Keillor
(1942-) Radio Host, Writer

The more people I meet, the more I like my cat.

Author Unknown

274

PETS

Insightful Observations on
THINGS CATS THINK

Cruel, but composed and bland,
Dumb, inscrutable and grand,
So Tiberius might have sat,
Had Tiberius been a cat.

 Matthew Arnold
(1822-1888) British Poet,
Critic

If cats spoke they would say things like,
"Hey, I don't see the problem here."

 Roy Blount, Jr.
(1941-) Humorist

In ancient times cats were worshipped as
gods; they have not forgotten this.

 Terry Pratchett
(1948-) British Humorist,
Author

I have noticed that what cats most
appreciate in a human being is not the
ability to produce food, which they take for
granted—but his or her entertainment
value.

 Geoffrey Household
(1900-1988) British Writer

Cats instinctively know the precise moment
their owners will awaken, and then they
wake them ten minutes sooner.

 Jim Davis
(1945-) Cartoonist; *Garfield*

The cat who purrs so sweetly cannot
fathom why her place in our bed has been
taken by this one who cries.

 Susan Eisenberg
(1950-) Author, Poet

If cats could talk, they wouldn't.

 Nan Porter
Present Day Author

Guide to Laughing Institute Honorees

The GTL institute recognizes those listed below for their
wit and wisdom, for helping others to laugh and learn about FAMILY,
and for the impact they have had on our culture.

(GTL Institute members are encouraged to further explore the works of those honored herein)

Laughing at Family Hall of Fame

Woody Allen
(1935-) Director, Actor,
Writer

Roseanne Barr
(1952-) Actress, Comedian,
Talk Show Host

Dave Barry
(1947-) Author Humorist

Milton Berle
(1908-2002) Comedian, Actor,
TV Personality

Erma Bombeck
(1927-1996) Humorist, Author

Stella Chess
(1914-) Author, Psychiatrist,
Professor of Child
Psychiatry

Bill Cosby
(1937-) Comedian, Actor

Marcelene Cox
20th Century Writer,
Columnist

Phyllis Diller
(1917-) Comedian, Actress,
Author

Reno Goodale
Present Day Comedian

Jean Kerr
(1922-2003) Writer,
Dramatist, Lyricist

Doug Larson
Present Day Cartoonist

Fran Lebowitz
(1950-) Writer, Humorist

Sam Levenson
(1911-1980) Humorist, Author

Phyllis McGinley
(1905-1978) Author, Poet

Ogden Nash
(1902-1971) Poet, Humorist

Anna Quindlen
(1953-) Novelist, Social Critic,
Columnist

Paul Reiser
(1957-) Actor, Writer,
Comedian

Joan Rivers
(1933-) Actress, Comedian

Rita Rudner
(1956-) Comedian

Margaret Smith
20th Century Comedian

Jerry Seinfeld
(1954-) Comedian, Actor,
Producer

Mark Twain
(1835-1910) Writer, Humorist

Steven Wright
(1955-) Actor, Writer,
Comedian

(The most quoted influencers in **The GTL at Family**)

Register membership and contribute "Insightful Observations" at
www.GuideToLaughing.com
277

Guide to Laughing Institute Honorees

Register membership and contribute "Insightful Observations" at
www.GuideToLaughing.com
279

Guide to Laughing Institute Honorees

Register membership and contribute "Insightful Observations" at

www.GuideToLaughing.com

Guide to Laughing Institute Influencers

The following individuals are recognized for their influence and example in shaping the *Guide to Laughing* handbooks, and for their contribution in helping others to laugh and learn about life.

Abby Goldstein
Adam Pergament
Adam Shankman
Adam Goldenberg
Adeo Ressi
Alan Wolpert
Alex Garbuio
Alex Lightman
Allen Tuller
Allesandro Tecchini
Amos Newman
Amy Eisenberg
Amy Karl
Amy Neunsinger
Amy Van Dyke
Andrew Schupak
Andy Goldschein
Andy Panzo
Angie Schwor
Ann Johnstad
Ann Magnuson
Ann Watson
Anna Gatterdam
Anne Neunsinger
Anthony Haden-Guest
April Uchitel
Ariane DeBonvoisin
Arnie Gullov-Singh
Ash Curtis
Barbara Blechman
Barbara Saunders
Becky Hamilton
Berkley Hanes
Betty Wasserman
Bianca Harzbecker
Bill Dolan
Bill Nelson
Bob Epstein
Bobette Cohn
Bob Holeman
Bonnie Solomon
Brad Beckerman
Brad Nye
Brett Brewer
Brian Seth Hurst
Bridget Sorenson
Brigitte Bourdeau
Brooke Carey
Brooks Martin
Bruce Fischer
Bruce Talan
Carl Bressler

Caroline Applegate
Caroline Sommers
Cathy Barsky
Catrina Gregory
Charles Sommer
Charles Goldschein
Charles Fedak
Chris Biller
Chris Dewolfe
Chris Lipp
Chris McCall
Chris Soumas
Chris Theberge
Christianne Cook
Christine Kozler
Christine Masterson
Chuck Fedak
Clare Kleinedler
Colin Sowa
Corey Reynolds
Courtney Nichols
Craig Filipacchi
Cynthia Cohen
Dan Bassett
Dan Pelson
Dan Loeb
Dana Albarella
Darren Romanelli
Darrin Higman
Dave Scarpa
David Bennahum
David Hershkovitz
David Hyman
David Spade
David Wilk
Deanna McDaniel
Debbie Levine
Debbie Snyder
Debbie Vitalie
Deigo Uchitel
Diana Liptak
Diane Snyder
Dominic Ianno
Don Gatterdam
Don Ressler
Donald Graham
Donni Briar
Donnie Osmond
Dr. Doug Hauck
Doug Rushkoff
Elise Newman
Elizabeth Whiting

Ella Kades
Elon Musk
EMILY
Eric Bogosian
Eric Troop
Eric B
Eric Barnes
Erin Cartwright
Evan Forster
Frank Keating
Frederic Bien
Gabriel Snyder
Garnie Nygren
Gary Dwardin
Gayle Shea
Genevive Moore
George Brandle
George Brightman
George Racz
Gerry McIntyre
Glenn Meyers
Gordon Gould
Greg Cass
Greg Clayman
Hal Sirowitz
Harry Magnie
Harvey Isaacs
Hayden Goldschein
Hayley Goldschein
Hedi Kim
Helen Roche
Henry Eshelman
Henry Shea
Henry E. Scott
Holly Schwarz
Howard Stern
Ian Shapolsky
Irwin Gold
Isadora Gullov-Singh
Jack Black
Jack Ohringer
Jackson Gold
Jacqui Samuels
Jade Li Kim
James Healy
Jamie Levy
Jane Hamilton
Jane Mount
Janice Gates
Jaqueline Moorby
Jason Calacanis
Jason Oates

Jay Goodman
Jay Rodriguez
Jay Tralese
JD Heilpren
Jeff Burke
Jeff Dachis
Jeff Henslin
Jeff Kravitz
Jeff Pollack
Jeff Stern
Jeff Weiss
Jeffery Gomanor
Jen Charat
Jennifer Anderson
Jennifer Enderlin
Jennifer Weis
Jenny Pelson
Jenny Landy
Jeremy Roberts
Jeremy Umland
Jerry Speigel
Jessica Felshman
Jilli Moss
Jillian Goldschein
Jim Panozza
Jim Wagner
Jim Wexler
Joan Barnes
Joanna Barnes
Joanna Kim
Joanna Scott
Jodi Rappaport
Joe Marich
Joe Robinson
Joel Gotler
Joel Kades
Joey Arias
Joey Cavella
John Kelly
John F. Kennedy Jr.
John Kjenner
John Lenard
John Mchugh
John Nicholson
John Warrin
Johnie Fodor
Jon Birge
Jon Marc Houmard
Jonathan Anastas
Jordan Crandel
Josette Wys
Josh Harris

Josh Rose
Josh Berman
Joyce Isaacs
JP Theberge
Judith Regan
Julie Halston
Justine Musk
Kaiama Glover
Kara Nygren
Karen Salmonsohn
Karen Stewart
Karen Switlyk
Kelly Rodriques
Kelly Jenkins
Ken Beckerman
Ken Campbell
Ken Rutkowski
Kerry Leibling
Kevin Kelly
Kevin Kent
Kevin Fox
Keiran Culkin
Kiersten Burke
Kim Kurilla
Kim Serafin
Korey Kolessa
Lady Bunny
Lancelot Link
Lane Jantzen
Laura Galloway
Laura Goldschein
Laura Shanahan
Laurel Wells
Lenore Pavlakos
Leslie Morava
Leslie France
Leslie Wells
Lindsay Goldschein
Lisa Baruch
Lisa Feldman
Lisa Gold
Lisa Goldschein
Lisa Kanino
Lisa Malin
Lisa Snyder
Lisa Thompson
Lisa Towel
Liz Heller
Liz Smith
Loleh Zayanderoudi
Lonnie Zeltzer
Lori Ann Vander Pluym
Lovis Hagopian
Luke Gatterdam
Lynn Maloney
Macalister Clabaugh
Mads Kornerup
Marc Landau

Marc Levey
Marc Scarpa
Marc Shaiman
Marc Von Arx
Marco Ilardi
Margaret Loeb
Margie Gilmore
Marie Nygren
Marisa Bowe
Mark Arrow
Mark Goodman
Mark Lindon
Mark Muscarella
Mark Tribe
Mark Williams
Marty Fienberg
Matt Coffin
Max Goldschein
Max Lodish
McGinn Shea
Melinda Farrell
Melissa Blau
Michael Barlow
Michael Dowling
Michael Kantrow
Michael Leopold
Michael Marx
Michael Diament
Michele Sebolt
Michelle Madansky
Milly Wasserman
Mike Maggio
Mike Schwarz
Mike Van Styne
Mike Kantrow
Mikhail Lapushner
Mikkel Bondeson
Mindy Espy
Molly McAlpine
Nancy Levie
Natalie Thomas
Natalie Warady
Natasha Esch
Natasha Tsarkova
Neil Gold
Neil Tiles
Neil Wolfson
Nicholas Butterworth
NOEL
Oduardo Lopez-Yanes
Owen Davis
Owen Masterson
Pam Leopold
PASH
Patricia Medved
Patrick Staves
Patti McConnel
Paul Rosenthal

Paul Zeltzer
Paula Heap
Paula Willaims
Paula Kowalczyk
Perry Hagopian
Peter Cohn
Peter Derasmo
Peter Flannigan
Peter Giblin
Peter Jennings
Phyliss Rosenthal
POPPIE
Quinn Nygren
Rabecca Lapinsky
Randi Steinback
Randy Horton
Raven O
Ray Khachatorian
Reed Davis
Rich Hull
RICHARD
Richard Laermer
Richard Titus
Ricky Rosenthal
Rob Fenter
Rob Fried
Rob Magnotta
Robert Blechman
Robert Gold
Robert I
Robert Patterson
Robert Tercek
Robin Lesser
Rowena Surloff
Roy Moraly
Ruby Egloff
Ruth Cousineau
Ryan Scott
Ryan Spencer
Sabastion Bernardo
Sam Ettus
Sam Humphries
Sandra Barker
Sarah Oscar
Scott Goldschein
Scott Mertz
Scott Wittman
Scott Babrour
Scott Heiferman
Sean Penn
Seth Goldstein
Shahyar Zayanderoudi
Shawn Thompson
Sherry Hilber
Shery Vine
SHERYL

Silas Bondeson
Simon Assaad
Siste Snyder
Spalding Gray
Spence Bovee
Spencer Tunick
Stacy Burka
Stan Topol
Stefan Langan
Stephan Walter
Stephen Baumer
Stephen Samuels
Steve Macon
Steve Berman
Steve Friedman
Steve Nygren
Steve Sackman
Steven Michaud
Stryker Lampe
Stuart Levy
Sunmin Park
Susan Swan
Sven Krong
Swan Paik
Tabitha Wilson
Ted Cohen
Ted Werth
Teddy Fiarillo
Tereza Predescu
Tim Giancarlo
Tim Ranson
Tim Hailand
Tim Rosta
Tina Goldschein
Tom Curtin
Tom Rusch
Tom Silverman
Tom Terpin
Tony Drockton
Tony Greenberg
Tonya Corrin
Torrie Dorrell
Trip Dubios
Tyler Gibgot
Uncle Burt
Vicki Samuels
Victor Harwood
Warren Zenna
Wayne Harburn
William Coplin
Willie Mack
Wylie Stecklow
Xeni Jardin
Yolande Yorke
Zach Leary
Zora Rasmussen

Register membership and contribute "Insightful Observations" at

www.GuideToLaughing.com

Member Registry

After making a "laughter connection" with someone, the owner of this book is authorized to register that person as a *Guide to Laughing Institute* member. This page serves as record of the date a laughter connection was made and a new member was inducted into the *Guide to Laughing Institute*.

How to register a new member:

1. Have new member agree to obligations on page 9 and choose a member title below
2. Record new member's name, signature, and date of laughter connection
3. Initialize this transaction
4. Welcome new member to the GTL Institute with a firm handshake and warm smile while maintaining eye contact
5. Inform all newly inducted members of their entitlement to all member privileges (See page 1)
6. For updates and information, register contact information at: GuideToLaughing.com

Member titles

Apostle of Humility	Goddess	Urban Shaman
Emissary of Optimism	Healing Minister	Spiritual Counselor
Flying Missionary	Mirth Messenger	Prof. of Absolute Reality

TITLE _____ TITLE _____ TITLE _____

NAME _____ NAME _____ NAME _____

SIGNATURE _____ SIGNATURE _____ SIGNATURE _____

DATE _____ INITIAL _____ DATE _____ INITIAL _____ DATE _____ INITIAL _____

TITLE _____   TITLE _____   TITLE _____

NAME _____   NAME _____   NAME _____

SIGNATURE _____   SIGNATURE _____   SIGNATURE _____

DATE _____ INITIAL _____   DATE _____ INITIAL _____   DATE _____ INITIAL _____

TITLE _____   TITLE _____   TITLE _____

NAME _____   NAME _____   NAME _____

SIGNATURE _____   SIGNATURE _____   SIGNATURE _____

DATE _____ INITIAL _____   DATE _____ INITIAL _____   DATE _____ INITIAL _____

TITLE _____   TITLE _____   TITLE _____

NAME _____   NAME _____   NAME _____

SIGNATURE _____   SIGNATURE _____   SIGNATURE _____

DATE _____ INITIAL _____   DATE _____ INITIAL _____   DATE _____ INITIAL _____

TITLE _____   TITLE _____   TITLE _____

NAME _____   NAME _____   NAME _____

SIGNATURE _____   SIGNATURE _____   SIGNATURE _____

DATE _____ INITIAL _____   DATE _____ INITIAL _____   DATE _____ INITIAL _____

TITLE _____   TITLE _____   TITLE _____

NAME _____   NAME _____   NAME _____

SIGNATURE _____   SIGNATURE _____   SIGNATURE _____

DATE _____ INITIAL _____   DATE _____ INITIAL _____   DATE _____ INITIAL _____

Founders Note

> *In my search for happiness, the most important discovery I made was that the things worth doing are the things we do for other people; the charming intersection of selfishness and virtue.*
>
> OSCAR HERMAN (1909-1980)   CO-FOUNDER, GTL INSTITUTE

My grandfather, Oscar Herman (1909–1980), a humorist and shoe salesman, inspired the creation of the *Guide to Laughing Institute* by the way he lived. His attitude and our conversations inspired a lifetime search to collect and organize humorous and insightful observations from influential people; and to share these thoughts so others can laugh and learn about life.

The observations in this book have been gathered and edited by GTL Institute members as they find humor and insight in their everyday lives. Each handbook is a compilation of thousands of member experiences including: reading religious texts, novels, reference books, road signs, newspapers, magazines, and instruction manuals; listening to songs on the radio; watching plays, interviews, lectures, movies, TV shows and from everyday conversations and experiences.

Since the formal organization began in 1993, hundreds of people—friends, writers, editors, artists, educators, doctors, executives, and celebrities—have helped shape the Guide to Laughing series.

Thank you for your participation, the *GTL Institute*'s message will continue to grow through the shared wit and laughter of its members.

Shawn Gold
Co-Founder, GTL Institute

Guide to Laughing Institute Founders

Oscar Herman (1909–1980) was an urban Jewish Will Rogers who never met a man he didn't like. He made a living by selling shoes and made a life by sharing his humor. Known as the Mayor of "F" street, a major section of Washington D.C. where he lived, he was revered for having friends of all creeds and colors. A generous champion of the neighborhood children, he often led parades of kids through the drug store candy isle, buying each marcher a treat. Impromptu performances of "Singing in the Rain" or "Alabami Bound," along with hilarious and insightful observations on love, sex, family, and life, were standard fare. Oscar believed the essence of life was connecting with people, and the key to connection was laughter. He was married to his wife Sarah for forty years when he died peacefully in his sleep in 1980. He is missed by the thousands of people whom he touched with his wit and his kindness.

Shawn Gold (1965–) Shawn lives his life with the same spirit and mission as his grandfather Oscar, helping people to laugh and learn about life. Professionally, he has used his understanding of laughter to build a career in helping people to adjust their attitudes. He developed advertising campaigns for some of Americas best known children's brands, wrote relationship advice columns for top women's magazines, and helped to create some of the most popular entertainment sites online. Personally, Shawn is overwhelmed by media and has a short attention span. He is keenly interested in finding the humor in life, thinking about it, and sharing it with others. His goal with *The Guide to Laughing* series is to convey insightful and amusing commentary with the greatest amount of thought per square word. He is married to photographer Amy Neunsinger, who he refers to as "an amazing human," and he is profoundly affected by the experience of being a new dad.

To Order Additional Copies

of The Guide to Laughing Institute Member Handbooks:

The Guide to Laughing at FAMILY
The Guide to Laughing at LOVE
The Guide to Laughing at SEX

Please visit

www.GuideToLaughing.com

or

Send a Check or Money Order for $12.95
per book (Free Shipping & Handling) to:

Guide to Laughing Orders
c/o Handy Logic Press
8033 Sunset Blvd., #490
Los Angeles, CA 90046

Coming in 2004-2005

The Guide to Laughing at EATING
The Guide to Laughing at HEALTH & AGE
The Guide to Laughing at OUR WORLD
The Guide to Laughing at YOURSELF
The Guide to Laughing at WORK

And if nothing else, always remember the words of the 21st Century philosopher and singer, Marie Osmond: "If you can look back on something and laugh at it, why not laugh about it now?"

THE GUIDE TO LAUGHING INSTITUTE